Through the Year Quilts

CREATED FOR LEISURE ARTS BY HOUSE OF WHITE BIRCHES

Contents

THROUGH THE YEAR QUILTS ©2003, 2001, 2000, 1999, 1998, 1997 House of White Birches, 306 East Parr Road, Berne, IN 46711, (260) 589-4000. Customer_Service@white-birches.com. Made in USA.

ISBN: 1-57486-346-0

Introduction

We are not sure why the passing of the seasons brings a sadness to so many people. Perhaps it is the uncertainty of the new or the loss of the old. Whatever the cause, there is nothing that will cure a case of the seasonal blues like making a quilt for the new season, and here are quilts to welcome and celebrate spring, summer, autumn and winter.

Winter Wreath

A delightful seasonal wreath quilt introduces each season. You may want to make each of the wreaths and change them with the season, or you might just pick your favorite. The beautiful spring flowers and the hummingbird wreath on page 4 will surely say spring. The roses on page 34 shine in the summer; autumn leaves and acorns on page 62 represent autumn, and holly leaves and berries on page 86 welcome winter.

Tulips & Nine Patch

If spring is your favorite season, celebrate the season with tulips in the Tulips & Nine Patch quilt on page 25.

A starry night at the beach is one of summer's pleasures, and with the paper piecing method you can re-create this glorious time in the beautiful Starry Night quilt on page 43.

Use assorted fabrics to create the leaves falling across the quilt in the Maple Leaf Harvest quilt on page 81, and you have certainly expressed the delight of autumn.

During those long winter months, when time is at a premium, why not brighten your house with the Winter Bears Quilt on page 96 or the Snowman Wall Quilt on page 111. Both small quilts can be quickly completed and enjoyed for many winters to come.

The wise say that "for every season there is a reason." Quilters say "for every season there should be a quilt!"

Spring Wreath

BY MARIAN SHENK

Beautiful spring flowers and a hummingbird all combine to introduce the spring quilts.

Spring Wreath

2" x 22"

E

A

Spring Wreath
Placement Diagram
26" x 26"

Spring Wreath

Project Specifications

Quilt Size: 26" x 26"

Fabric & Batting

- ¼ yard yellow print
- ¾ yard cream-on-cream print
- Scraps green, bright pink, peach, light yellow, dark yellow and blue prints
- Scraps light gray, dark gray, gold, peach and blue solids
- Backing 30" x 30"
- Batting 30" x 30"
- 4 yards self-made or purchased binding

Supplies & Tools

- All-purpose thread to match fabrics
- Off-white quilting thread
- 1 skein each brown and gold 6-strand embroidery floss
- Black indelible pen
- ½ yard ⅛"-wide brown bias tape
- Basic sewing tools and supplies and water-erasable marker or pencil

Instructions

1. Prepare templates using pattern pieces given. Cut as directed on each piece, adding a ⅛"–¼" seam allowance all around each appliqué piece when cutting for hand appliqué.

2. Cut a 16½" x 16½" square cream-on-cream print for background. Fold in half on both sides and crease to mark centers.

3. Copy full-size pattern onto a large piece of paper. Pin on a window. Tape background block over pattern, using center crease marks as a guide. Transfer full-size pattern onto background square using a water-erasable marker or pencil.

4. Pin pieces in place in numerical order using marked lines as a guide, overlapping as shown on pattern.

5. Hand-appliqué pieces in place using all-purpose thread to match fabrics. Embroider straight stitches using 2 strands brown embroidery floss to make flower center lines as indicated on pattern pieces. Straight-stitch bird's beak using 2 strands gold embroidery floss. Make dot for bird's eye using black indelible pen.

6. Sew a cream-on-cream print B to a yellow print B; repeat for four B units. Repeat for four BR units.

7. Sew D to two adjacent sides of C; add a yellow print B and BR as shown in Figure 1; repeat for four units.

Figure 1
Sew D to 2 adjacent sides of C;
add a yellow print B and BR.

Spring Wreath

8. Sew a B unit and a BR unit to opposite ends of the B-C-D unit as shown in Figure 2; repeat for four units.

Figure 2
Sew a B unit and a BR unit to
opposite ends of the B-C-D unit.

9. Sew a pieced unit to opposite sides of the appliquéd center as shown in Figure 3. Press seams toward the appliquéd center.

Figure 3
Sew a pieced unit to opposite
sides of the appliquéd center.

10. Sew an A piece to each end of the remaining two pieced units; sew to the remaining sides of the pieced and appliquéd center. Press seams toward the appliquéd center.

11. Cut four strips cream-on-cream print 2½" x 22½". Sew a strip to opposite sides of the pieced and appliquéd center; press seams toward strips.

12. Sew E to each end of the remaining two strips. Sew a strip to the remaining sides of the pieced and appliquéd center; press seams toward strips.

13. Sandwich batting between completed top and prepared backing piece. Pin or baste layers together to hold flat.

14. Hand-quilt around each appliquéd shape and in the ditch of all pieced seams using off-white quilting thread.

15. Mark quilting design given in cream-on-cream print border and background corners using water-erasable marker or pencil. Hand-quilt on marked lines using off-white quilting thread.

16. When quilting is complete, trim edges even; remove pins or basting. Bind edges with self-made or purchased binding to finish.

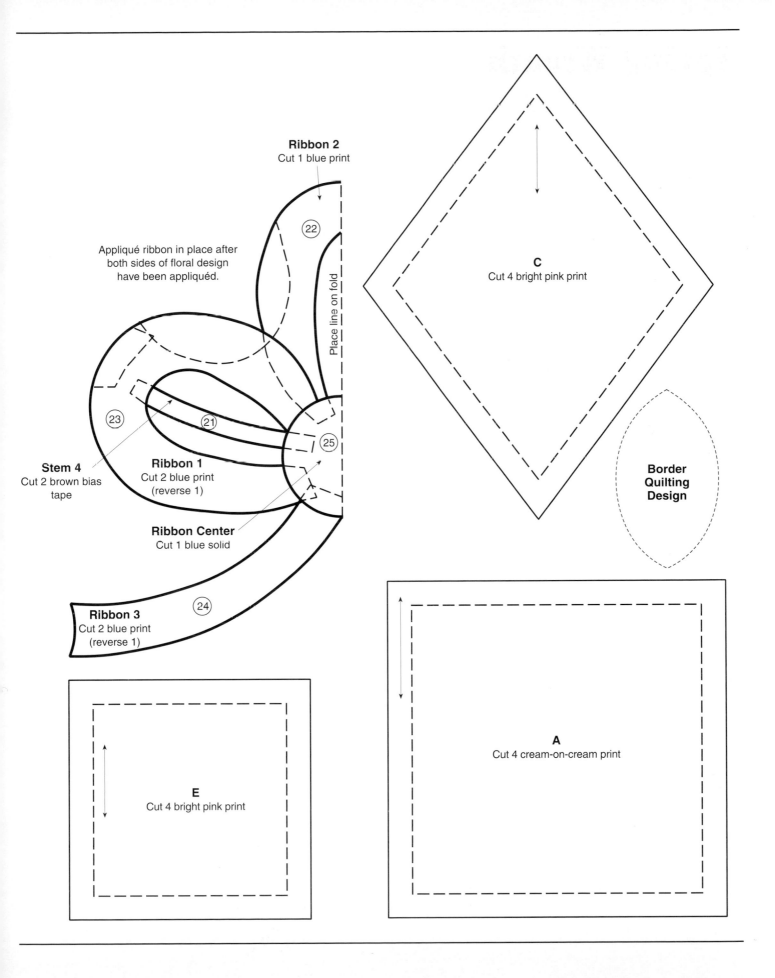

Ribbon 2
Cut 1 blue print

Appliqué ribbon in place after both sides of floral design have been appliquéd.

Place line on fold

22

C
Cut 4 bright pink print

Border Quilting Design

23

21

25

Stem 4
Cut 2 brown bias tape

Ribbon 1
Cut 2 blue print (reverse 1)

Ribbon Center
Cut 1 blue solid

24

Ribbon 3
Cut 2 blue print (reverse 1)

A
Cut 4 cream-on-cream print

E
Cut 4 bright pink print

Spring Wreath

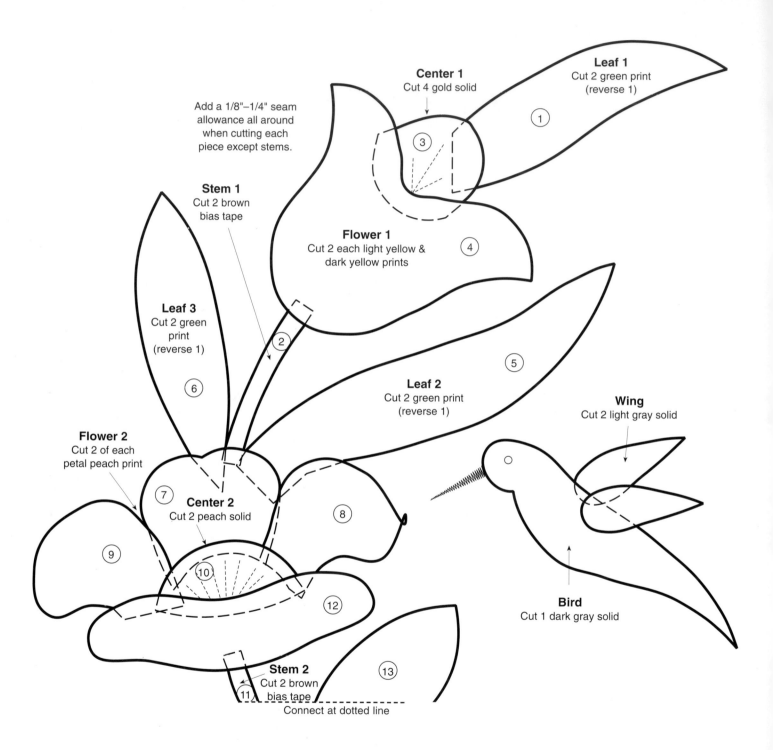

Add a 1/8"–1/4" seam allowance all around when cutting each piece except stems.

Center 1
Cut 4 gold solid

Leaf 1
Cut 2 green print
(reverse 1)

Stem 1
Cut 2 brown
bias tape

Flower 1
Cut 2 each light yellow &
dark yellow prints

Leaf 3
Cut 2 green
print
(reverse 1)

Leaf 2
Cut 2 green print
(reverse 1)

Wing
Cut 2 light gray solid

Flower 2
Cut 2 of each
petal peach print

Center 2
Cut 2 peach solid

Bird
Cut 1 dark gray solid

Stem 2
Cut 2 brown
bias tape
Connect at dotted line

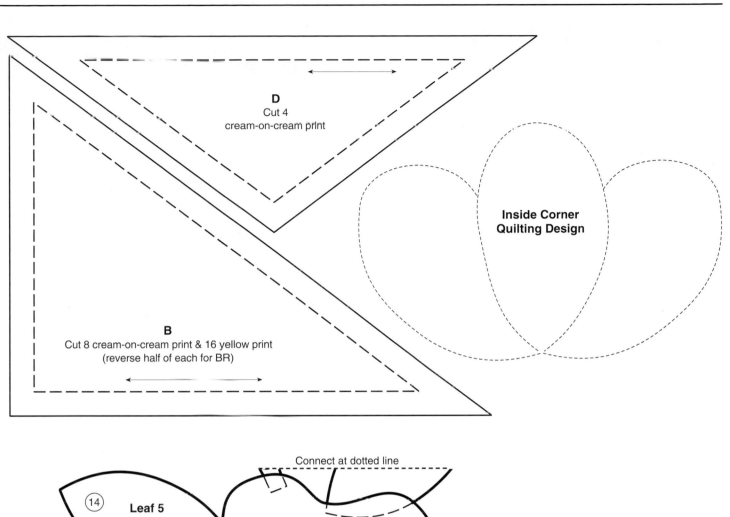

D
Cut 4
cream-on-cream print

**Inside Corner
Quilting Design**

B
Cut 8 cream-on-cream print & 16 yellow print
(reverse half of each for BR)

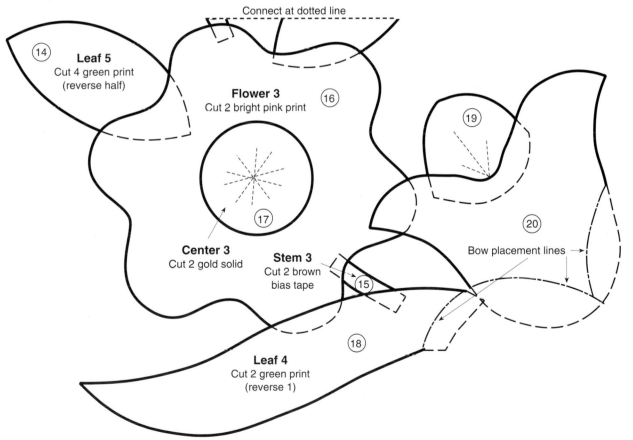

Connect at dotted line

⑭ **Leaf 5**
Cut 4 green print
(reverse half)

Flower 3
Cut 2 bright pink print ⑯

⑲

⑳

Center 3
Cut 2 gold solid ⑰

Stem 3
Cut 2 brown
bias tape ⑮

Bow placement lines →

⑱

Leaf 4
Cut 2 green print
(reverse 1)

Dogwood

BY BONNIE S. GHEESLING

Those beautiful spring dogwood blossoms bloom on this quilt, and when you make this quilt, you will keep those blossoms all year long. The quilt in the photograph was hand-appliquéd and hand-quilted. The instructions here are for machine appliqué because we like quicker projects. If you prefer to use hand methods, add a seam allowance to the pieces when cutting and eliminate the fusible transfer web and fabric stabilizer.

Dogwood

Dogwood
Placement Diagram
70" x 84"

Dogwood

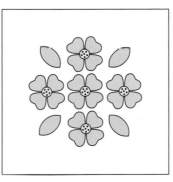

Dogwood
15" x 15" Block

Project Specifications

Quilt Size: 70" x 84"

Block Size: 15" x 15"

Number of Blocks: 15

Fabric & Batting

- ¼ yard yellow solid
- 1¼ yards light green solid
- 1⅝ yards light pink solid
- 4¼ yards white solid
- Light pink solid backing 80" x 95"
- Batting 75" x 89"

Supplies & Tools

- All-purpose thread to match fabric
- 6 yards fusible transfer web
- 6 yards fabric stabilizer
- 2 skeins tan 6-strand embroidery floss
- ¼" bias bar
- Basic sewing tools and supplies

Instructions

1. Prepare templates for appliqué shapes using pattern pieces given.

2. Bond fusible transfer web to the yellow solid, ⅜ yard light green solid and 1⅝ yards light pink solid referring to manufacture's instructions.

3. Trace flower and leaf shapes onto paper side of fused fabrics as directed on patterns for number to cut. Cut out shapes on traced lines; remove paper backing.

4. Cut one strip white solid 8½" by length of fabric; set aside for borders. Cut 15 squares white solid 15½" x 15½". Fold each square and crease to mark centers.

5. Center and arrange five dogwood flower motifs and four leaves on each block using crease lines as guides referring to Figure 1. When satisfied with placement, fuse in place.

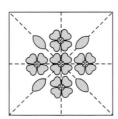

Figure 1
Center and arrange 5
dogwood flower motifs
and 4 leaves on each
block using crease
lines as guides.

Dogwood

6. Cut fabric stabilizer to fit behind fused shapes. Machine-appliqué shapes in place using matching all-purpose thread and a straight stitch close to cut edge of each piece. Remove fabric stabilizer.

7. Join three blocks to make a row; press seams in one direction. Repeat for five rows. Join the rows; press seams in one direction.

8. Cut two strips white solid 8½" x 75½" from strip cut in step 4. Sew a strip to opposite long sides of the pieced center; press seams toward strips.

9. Cut a 10" x 10" square light green solid. Cut into ¾" bias strips as shown in Figure 2. You will need a total of 3 yards bias.

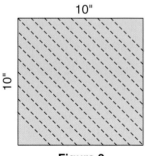

10"

10"

Figure 2
Cut into 3/4" bias strips.

10. Fold each bias strip in half along length with wrong sides together; stitch with wrong sides together; stitch with a ⅛" seam. Insert the ¼"

bias bar into tube as shown in Figure 3; press. Cut into 4½" segments; you will need 20 segments.

Figure 3
Insert a 1/4" bias bar into tube.

11. Center and fuse one flower motif at the intersections of blocks as shown in Figure 4; repeat on block/border strip intersections. Appliqué in place as in step 6.

Figure 4
Center and fuse 1 flower motif at the intersections of blocks and borders.

12. Arrange and fuse flowers and leaves with bias stems on white border stripes, centering two flower motifs opposite each block referring to the Placement Diagram. Appliqué in place as in step 6.

13. Cut and piece two strips each 2½" x 61½" and 2½" x 79½" light green solid. Sew the shorter strips

to the top and bottom and longer strips to opposite long sides; press seams toward strips.

14. Center and sandwich batting between completed top and prepared backing; pin or baste layers together to hold flat. *Note: Be sure that 5" of batting and 8" of backing extend beyond quilt top on all sides.*

15. Quilt as desired by hand or machine. When quilting is complete, remove pins or basting.

16. Trim batting to 2½" beyond edges of quilt top all around.

17. Trim backing to 2¾" beyond batting edges all around; turn under ¼" of backing and press.

18. Fold backing over to front side, mitering corners and covering raw edges of light green print border stripes; press. Hand- or machine-stitch in place.

19. Using 3 strands tan embroidery floss, make 6–8 French knots in the yellow solid center of each flower. *Note: More detailed embroidery may be added to flower petals if desired.*

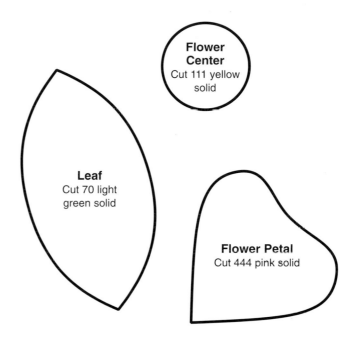

Flower Center
Cut 111 yellow solid

Leaf
Cut 70 light green solid

Flower Petal
Cut 444 pink solid

Stepping Stars

BY JILL REBER

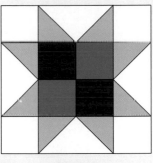

Block A
8" x 8" Block
Make 22

Star motifs of all types are very popular with quiltmakers, but many of them are complicated and difficult to piece. Simple Four-Patch blocks make up this easy star design. Stars are always lovely spread out across an inviting spring sky.

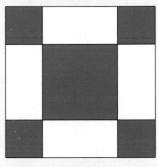

Block B
8" x 8" Block
Make 17

Stepping Stars

Project Specifications

Quilt Size: 60" x 76"

Block Size: 8" x 8"

Number of Blocks: 35

Fabric & Batting

- ¼ yard medium blue print 1
- ¾ yard medium blue print 2
- 1¼ yards each light blue and dark blue prints
- 3 yards muslin
- Backing 64" x 80"
- Batting 64" x 80"
- 8 yards self-made or purchased binding

Supplies & Tools

- All-purpose thread to match fabrics
- Basic sewing tools and supplies, 8" x 24" ruler, rotary cutter and mat

Block A

1. Cut seven light blue print strips 2⅞" by fabric width. Cut strips into 2⅞" square segments; repeat for 88 squares. Cut each square in half on one diagonal to make 176 A triangles.

2. Cut six strips muslin 2½" by fabric width. Cut into 2½" square segments; repeat for 88 B squares.

Stepping Stars

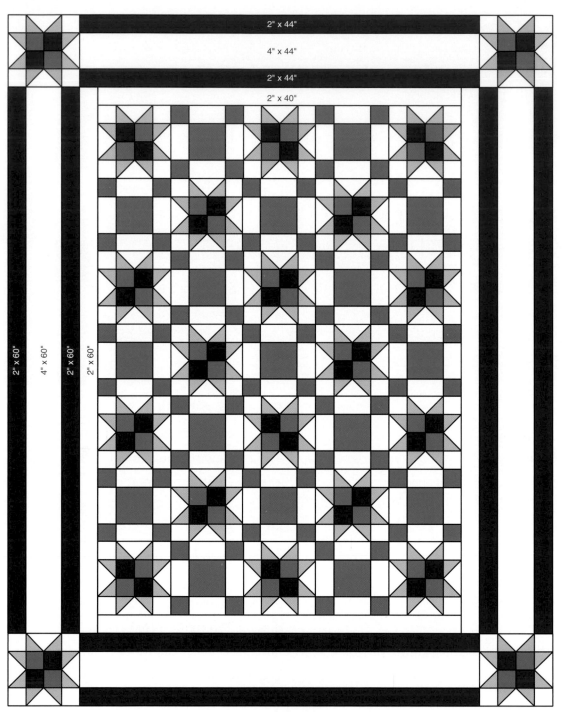

Stepping Stars
Placement Diagram
60" x 76"

3. Cut three strips muslin 5¼" by fabric width. Cut into 5¼" square segments. Cut each square in half on both diagonals to make four C triangles from each square. You will need 88 C triangles.

4. Cut three strips each medium blue print 1 and dark blue print 2½" by fabric width.

5. Sew a medium blue print 1 strip to a dark blue print strip along length; repeat for three strip sets. Press seams toward dark blue print strips. Subcut strips into 2½" segments.

6. Join two segments made in step 5 to make a Four-Patch unit as shown in Figure 1; repeat for 22 Four-Patch units.

Figure 1
Join segments to make
a Four-Patch unit.

7. Cut two strips each medium blue print 2 and muslin 4½" by fabric width. Cut four strips each medium blue print 2 and muslin 2½" by fabric width.

Figure 2
Sew 2 A triangles to C to make
a Flying Geese unit.

8. Sew a B square to each end of a Flying Geese unit as shown in Figure 3; repeat for 44 units.

Figure 3
Sew a B square to each end of a
Flying Geese unit.

9. Sew a Flying Geese unit to opposite sides of a Four-Patch unit; repeat for 22 units.

10. Arrange pieced units in rows. Join units in rows; join rows to complete one block as shown in Figure 4. Press; repeat for 22 A Blocks. Set aside.

Figure 4
Join rows to
complete 1 A block.

Block B

1. Cut two strips each medium blue print 2 and muslin 4½" by fabric width. Cut four strips each medium blue print 2 and muslin 2½" by fabric width.

Stepping Stars

2. Sew a 2½" muslin strip to each long side of a 4½" medium blue print 2 strip; press seams toward the medium blue print 2 strips. Repeat for two strip sets.

3. Subcut strip sets into 4½" segments; you will need 17 segments.

4. Sew a 2½"-wide medium blue print 2 strip to each long side of a 4½"-wide muslin strip; press seams toward medium blue print 2 strips. Repeat for two strip sets.

5. Subcut strip sets into 2½" segments; you will need 34 segments.

6. Arrange the segments as shown in Figure 5; join to complete one block. Press; repeat for 17 B Blocks.

Figure 5
Join segments to
make 1 B block.

Quilt Construction

1. Join three A Blocks with two B Blocks to make a row as shown in Figure 6; repeat for four rows. Press seams toward B Blocks.

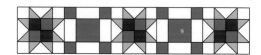

Figure 6
Join 3 A blocks with 2 B blocks to make a row.

2. Join three B Blocks with two A Blocks to make a row as shown in Figure 7; repeat for three rows. Press seams toward B Blocks.

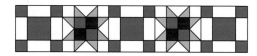

Figure 7
Join 3 B blocks with 2 A blocks to make a row.

3. Lay rows out referring to Placement Diagram for arrangement. Join rows to complete pieced center. Press seams in one direction.

4. Cut two strips muslin 2½" x 40½"; sew a strip to the top and bottom of the pieced center. Press seams toward strips.

5. Cut and piece muslin to make two strips each 2½" x 60½". Sew a strip to each long side; press seams toward strips.

6. Cut and piece four strips dark blue print 2½" x 44½" and two strips muslin 4½" x 44½". Sew a muslin strip between two dark blue print strips; press seams toward dark blue print strips. Repeat for second strip set. Sew a strip set to the top and bottom of the pieced center; press seams toward dark blue print strips.

7. Cut and piece four strips dark blue print 2½" x 60½" and two strips muslin 4½" x 60½". Sew a muslin strip between two dark blue print strips; press seams toward dark blue print strips. Repeat for second strip set.

8. Sew an A Block to each end of each strip set.

Sew strip sets to the long sides of the pieced center; press seams toward dark blue print strips.

9. Mark a chosen quilting design on finished quilt top.

10. Sandwich batting between prepared backing and completed quilt top. Pin or baste layers together to hold flat for quilting.

11. Quilt on marked lines and as desired by hand or machine.

13. When quilting is complete, trim edges even. Bind with self-made or purchased binding to finish.

Tulips & Nine-Patch

BY NANCY BRENAN DANIEL

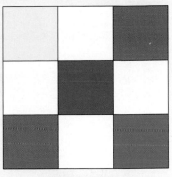

Nine-Patch
6" x 6" Block

Nothing represents spring the way the tulip does. Once the tulips start popping up in the garden, we know that winter is over. In this quilt, Nine-Patch blocks act as a background for the Tulip blocks, and the bright spring colors carry the promise of sunshine and warmer days.

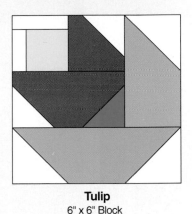

Tulip
6" x 6" Block

Tulips & Nine-Patch

Project Specifications

Quilt Size: 27" x 39"
Block Size: 6" x 6"
Number of Blocks: 7 Nine-Patch and 8 Tulip

Fabric & Batting

- 1 strip 2½" x 18" each rose, yellow and blue prints
- 2 strips 2½" x 18" lavender print
- ⅛ yard green solid
- ⅙ yard purple and yellow print
- ¼ yard light purple print
- ¼ yard total green prints
- ½ yard muslin
- ½ yard large floral print

- Backing 31" x 43"
- Batting 31" x 43"
- 4 yards self-made or purchased binding

Supplies & Tools

- Neutral color all-purpose thread
- Off-white quilting thread
- Basic sewing tools and supplies, rotary cutter, ruler and cutting mat

Making Nine-Patch Blocks

1. Cut four strips muslin 2½" x 18".

2. Sew a blue print strip to a muslin strip to a lavender print strip; press seams away from the muslin strip.

Tulips & Nine-Patch

3" x 21"

1 1/2" x 18"

3" x 39"

1 1/2" x 33"

Tulips & Nine-Patches
Placement Diagram
27" x 39"

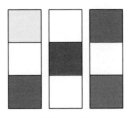

Figure 2
Arrange the segments to
make a Nine-Patch block.

3. Sew a rose print strip between two muslin strips; press seams away from muslin.

4. Sew a yellow print strip to a muslin strip to a lavender print strip; press seams away from the muslin strip.

5. Cut each strip set into 2½" segments as shown in Figure 1. You will need seven segments from each strip.

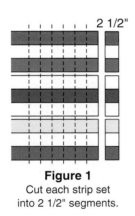

2 1/2"

Figure 1
Cut each strip set
into 2 1/2" segments.

6. Arrange the segments as shown in Figure 2 to make a Nine-Patch block. Join segments to complete one block; repeat for seven blocks. Press seams in one direction.

Making Tulip Blocks

1. Cut the following from muslin: eight 1" x 2" rectangles for A; eight 1" x 2½" rectangles for B; 16 squares 2" x 2" for C; and 24 squares 2½" x 2½" for D.

2. Cut eight squares yellow print 2" x 2" for E.

3. Cut eight squares purple print 2½" x 2½" for F and eight rectangles purple print 2½" x 4½" for G.

4. Cut eight squares green solid 2" x 2" for H.

5. Cut eight rectangles green print each 2½" x 4½" for I and 2½" x 6½" for J.

Tulips & Nine-Patch

6. To piece one block, sew A to E; add B to adjacent side of E as shown in Figure 3.

Figure 3
Add B to adjacent
side of E.

7. Sew F to the A-B-E unit; add G as shown in Figure 4.

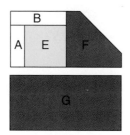

Figure 4
Sew F to the
A-B-E unit; add G.

8. Place a C square on the corner of F; sew on the diagonal of the square as shown in Figure 5; trim excess ¼" from seam. Press C to make a triangle corner on F as shown in Figure 6.

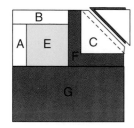

Figure 5
Place a C square on the corner
of F; sew on the diagonal of the
square; trim to 1/4"

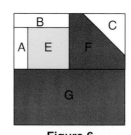

Figure 6
Press C to make a
triangle corner on F.

9. Repeat with C and H on G as shown in Figure 7.

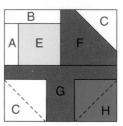

Figure 7
Sew C and H
to G as shown.

10. Sew I and J to the pieced unit as shown in Figure 8. Sew D to three corners as in step 8 and referring to Figure 9 to complete one block. Repeat for eight blocks.

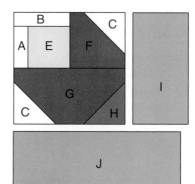

Figure 8
Sew I and J to the
pieced unit as shown.

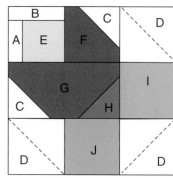

Figure 9
Sew D to 3 corners; trim and
press to complete block.

Quilt Assembly & Finishing

1. Join two Tulip blocks with a Nine-Patch block to make a Tulip row as shown in Figure 10; press seams in one direction. Repeat for three Tulip rows.

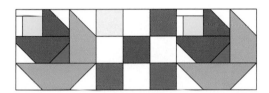

Figure 10
Join 2 Tulip blocks with a Nine-Patch block
to make a Tulip row.

2. Join two Nine-Patch blocks with a Tulip block to make a Nine-Patch row as shown in Figure 11; press seams in one direction. Repeat for two rows.

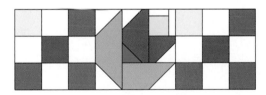

Figure 11
Join 2 Nine-Patch blocks with a Tulip
block to make a Nine-Patch row.

3. Join rows beginning and ending with a Tulip row; press seams in one direction.

4. Cut two strips each light purple print 2" x 18½" and 2" x 33½". Sew the shorter strips to the top and bottom and longer strips to opposite long sides; press seams toward strips.

5. Cut two strips each large floral print 3½" x 21½" and 3½" x 39½". Sew the shorter strips to the top and bottom and longer strips to opposite long sides; press seams toward strips.

6. Sandwich batting between completed top and prepared backing piece. Pin or baste layers together to hold flat.

7. Quilt as desired by hand or machine using off-white quilting thread. When quilting is complete, remove pins or basting; trim edges even.

8. Bind edges with self-made or purchased binding to finish.

Sweet as Sugar

BY JILL REBER

Pinwheels are easy and fun to make, especially if you follow the hint given in the instructions for making seams lie flatter. This charming quilt could be used as a lap quilt, a wall quilt or a baby quilt, and it is the perfect project for someone who has been sewing a long time and has lots of dark and light scraps of fabric.

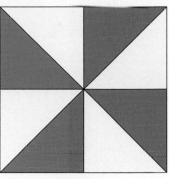

Pinwheel
6" x 6" Block

Sweet as Sugar

Project Specifications

Quilt Size: 42" x 54"

Block Size: 6" x 6"

Number of Blocks: 39

Fabric & Batting

- ½ yard each dark and light scraps
- 1½ yards border fabric
- Backing 46" x 58"
- Batting 46" x 58"
- 6 yards self-made or purchased binding

Supplies & Tools

- Neutral color all-purpose thread
- 1 spool matching quilting thread
- Basic sewing tools and supplies, rotary cutter, ruler and cutting mat

Instructions

1. For each block cut two squares each dark and light scraps 3⅞" x 3⅞". Cut each square in half on one diagonal to make triangles. You will need 78 squares each from light and dark scraps to complete project.

2. Sew a dark triangle to a light triangle along diagonal sides to make a square as shown in Figure 1; repeat for four triangle/squares. Press seams toward dark triangle; trim seam points even with pieced square.

Figure 1
Join 2 triangles to make trlangle/square.

Sweet as Sugar

6" x 30"

6" x 42"

Sweet as Sugar
Placement Diagram
42" x 54"

3. Arrange the four triangle/squares to make a block as shown in Figure 2; join two squares twice; press seams in opposite directions. Join the pieced units to complete one block. Repeat cutting and piecing to make 39 blocks.

Figure 2
Arrange triangle/squares in
2 rows of 2 units each.

4. Arrange the blocks in seven rows of five blocks each. Join in rows; join rows to complete pieced center and press.

5. Cut two strips border fabric 6½" x 30½" and two strips 6½" x 42½". Sew the shorter strips to the top and bottom. Sew a pieced block to each end of the longer strips and sew to opposite sides; press seams toward strips.

6. Sandwich batting between completed top and prepared backing piece. Pin or baste layers together to hold flat. Quilt as desired by hand or machine.

7. When quilting is complete, trim edges even. Bind with self-made or purchased binding to finish.

Hint: To help make seams in the block lie flatter, try this trick. Make the block, pressing seams as directed in pattern instructions. When joining two units, press one seam to the left and one to the right. Sew the seam across joining the four units together. After stitching, pick out a few stitches in the center allowing you to flip the seam in the other direction forming a pinwheel in the center of the block as shown in Figure 3.

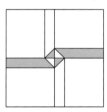

Figure 3
Press center seams as
shown to reduce bulk.

Summer Wreath

BY MARIAN SHENK

Roses that bloom all summer
introduce our summer quilts!

Summer Wreath

2" x 22"

2" x 2"

Summer Wreath
Placement Diagram
26" x 26"

Summer Wreath

Project Specifications

Quilt Size: 26" x 26"

Fabric & Batting

- ¼ yard deep rose print
- ¾ yard cream-on-cream print
- Scraps rose, dark rose, gold and green prints or solids
- Backing 30" x 30"
- Batting 30" x 30"
- 3¼ yards self-made or purchased binding

Supplies & Tools

- All-purpose thread to match fabrics
- Off-white quilting thread
- 1 package ⅛"-wide green bias tape
- Basic sewing tools and supplies and water-erasable marker or pencil

Instructions

1. Prepare templates using pattern pieces given. Cut as directed on each piece, adding a ⅛"–¼" seam allowance all around each appliqué piece when cutting for hand appliqué.

2. Cut a 16½" x 16½" square cream-on-cream print for background. Fold in half on both sides and crease to mark centers.

3. Copy full-size pattern onto a large piece of paper. Tape on a window. Tape background block over pattern, using center crease marks as a guide. Transfer full-size pattern onto background square using a water-erasable marker or pencil.

4. Pin pieces in place in numerical order using marked lines as a guide, overlapping as shown on pattern. Use narrow bias tape for stem pieces.

5. Hand-appliqué pieces in place using all-purpose thread to match fabrics.

6. Sew D and DR to one end of A as shown in Figure 1; repeat for eight units. Add C to one side of each unit as shown in Figure 2; join two A-D-C units to make one side unit. Repeat for four side units.

Figure 1
Sew D and DR to 1 end of A.

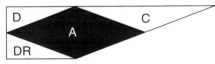
Figure 2
Add C to 1 side of each unit.

7. Sew E to each side of B; repeat for four units.

8. Sew an A-D-C unit to two opposite sides of the appliquéd center. Sew a B-E unit to each end of the remaining two side units. Sew one unit to each remaining side of the appliquéd center. Press seams toward strips.

Summer Wreath

9. Cut four strips cream-on-cream print 2½" x 22½". Sew a strip to two opposite sides of the pieced and appliquéd center; press seams toward strips.

10. Sew F to each end of the remaining two strips. Sew a strip to the remaining sides of the pieced and appliquéd center; press seams toward strips.

11. Sandwich batting between completed top and prepared backing piece. Pin or baste layers together to hold flat.

12. Hand-quilt around each appliquéd shape and in the ditch of all pieced seams using off-white quilting thread.

13. Mark quilting design given on cream-on-cream print border and background corners using water-erasable marker or pencil. Hand-quilt on marked lines using off-white quilting thread.

14. When quilting is complete, trim edges even; remove pins or basting. Bind edges with self-made or purchased binding to finish.

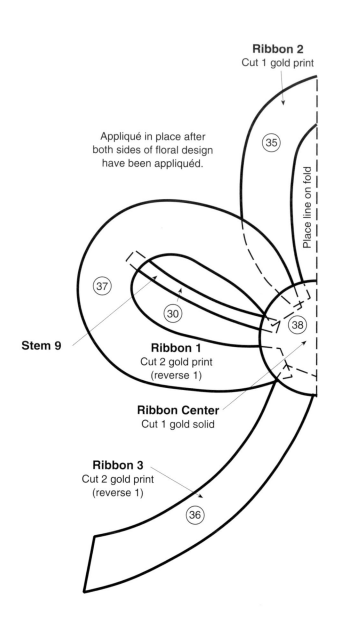

Ribbon 2
Cut 1 gold print

Appliqué in place after both sides of floral design have been appliquéd.

Place line on fold

35

Stem 9

37

30

38

Ribbon 1
Cut 2 gold print
(reverse 1)

Ribbon Center
Cut 1 gold solid

Ribbon 3
Cut 2 gold print
(reverse 1)

36

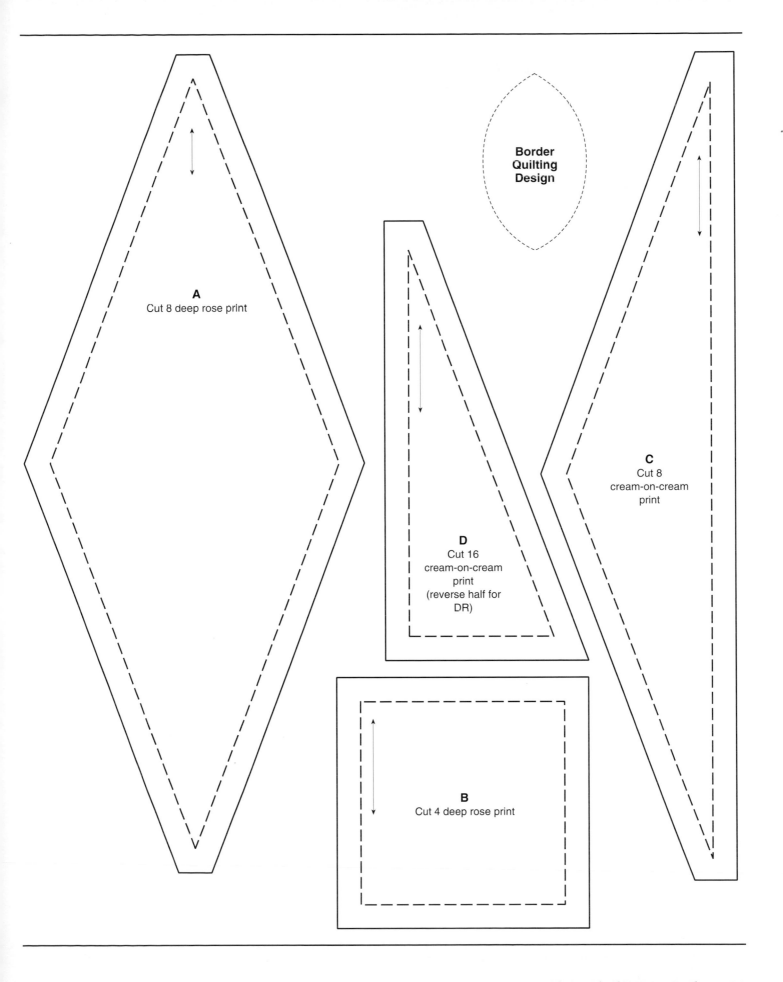

A
Cut 8 deep rose print

Border Quilting Design

C
Cut 8
cream-on-cream
print

D
Cut 16
cream-on-cream
print
(reverse half for DR)

B
Cut 4 deep rose print

Summer Wreath

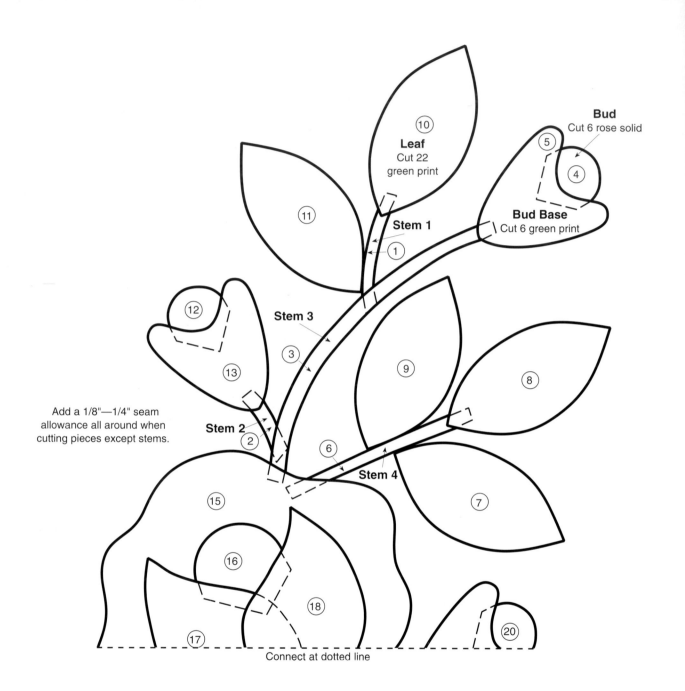

Leaf
Cut 22
green print

Bud
Cut 6 rose solid

Stem 1

Bud Base
Cut 6 green print

Stem 3

Add a 1/8"—1/4" seam
allowance all around when
cutting pieces except stems.

Stem 2

Stem 4

Connect at dotted line

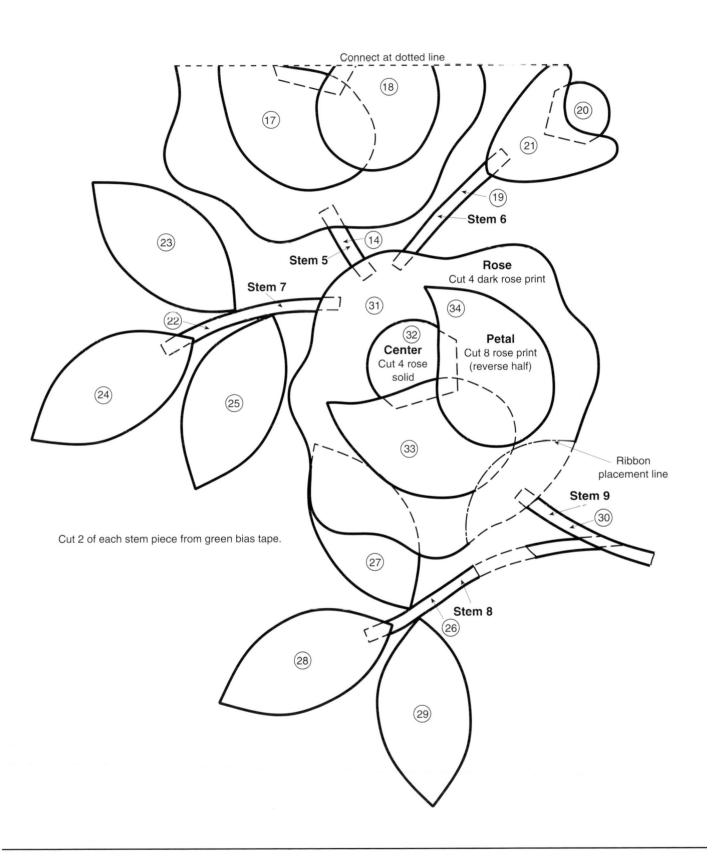

Connect at dotted line

⑱

⑰

⑳

㉑

⑲

Stem 6

㉓

⑭

Stem 5

Rose
Cut 4 dark rose print

Stem 7

㉒

㉛

㉞

㉜

Petal
Cut 8 rose print
(reverse half)

Center
Cut 4 rose
solid

㉔

㉕

㉝

Ribbon
placement line

Stem 9

㉚

Cut 2 of each stem piece from green bias tape.

㉗

Stem 8

㉖

㉘

㉙

Summer Wreath

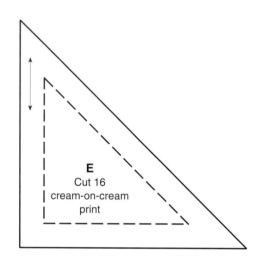

E
Cut 16
cream-on-cream
print

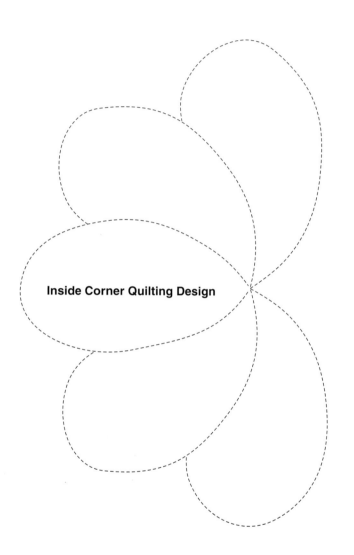

Inside Corner Quilting Design

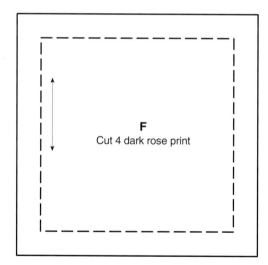

F
Cut 4 dark rose print

Starlight Quilt

BY JOHANNA WILSON

A great quilt for the lazy days of summer! The Star blocks in this quilt are made in a unique method, rather than the traditional block construction. It's a quick, accurate and easy method, but it is a bit like putting together a puzzle. The stars are made in units, and the final star designs won't show until all of the units are pieced together. So be patient; eventually the stars jump out.

Starlight Quilt

Project Specifications

Quilt Size: 58" x 66"

Fabric & Batting

- ⅓ yard rose print
- ¾ yard burgundy print
- 1⅓ yards cream print
- 2½ yards red/cream plaid
- Backing 62" x 70"
- Batting 62" x 70"
- 7¼ yards self-made or purchased binding

Supplies & Tools

- Neutral color all-purpose thread
- Basic sewing tools and supplies

Instructions

1. Cut three strips 4½" by fabric width cream print; subcut strips into 2½" units to make A rectangles. You will need 48 A rectangles.

2. Cut two strips 6½" by fabric width cream print; subcut strips into 2½" units to make B rectangles. You will need 24 B rectangles.

3. Cut two strips 6½" by fabric width cream print; subcut into 4½" units to make C rectangles. You will need 12 C rectangles.

4. Cut one strip 4½" by fabric width cream print; subcut into 4½" square units to make D squares. You will need eight D squares.

Starlight Quilt

5. Cut eight strips 2½" by fabric width burgundy print; subcut strips into 2½" square units for E squares. You will need 128 E squares.

6. Cut two strips 4½" by fabric width rose print; subcut strips into 4½" square units for F squares. You will need 16 F squares.

7. To make one A unit, place an E square on A with right sides together; stitch on one diagonal as shown in Figure 1. Trim ¼" beyond stitching line as shown in Figure 2. Repeat with a second E square as shown in Figure 3.

Figure 1
Place an E square on A
with right sides together;
stitch on 1 diagonal.

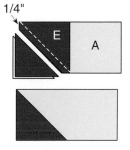

Figure 2
Trim 1/4" beyond
stitching line; press.

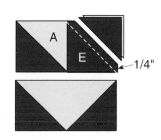

Figure 3
Place a second E square
on the adjacent corner of A.

8. Trim as in Figure 2 and press; repeat for 32 A units.

9. To make one B-C unit, stitch an E square to each corner of C and trim as in step 7 and referring to Figure 4. Sew B to opposite long sides as shown in Figure 5 to complete one B-C unit; repeat for 12 B-C units.

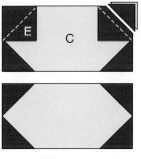

Figure 4
Sew E to each corner
of C; trim and press.

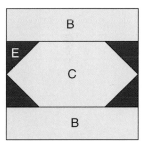

Figure 5
Sew B to opposite long sides
to complete 1 B-C unit.

10. To make one A-D unit, stitch an E square to two adjacent corners of D and trim as in step 7 and referring to Figure 6. Add A to opposite sides as shown in Figure 7; press to complete one A-D unit. Repeat for eight A-D units.

Starlight Quilt

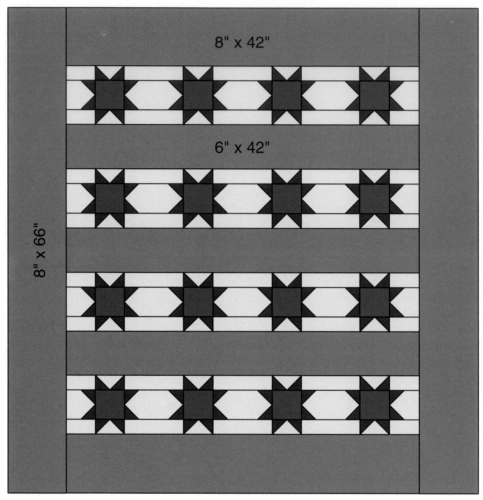

Starlight Quilt
Placement Diagram
58" x 66"

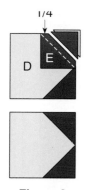

Figure 6
Stitch an E square to 2
adjacent corners of D and trim.

Figure 7
Add A to opposite
sides; press to
complete 1 A-D unit.

11. Sew an A unit to two opposite sides of F as shown in Figure 8 to complete an A-F unit; repeat for 16 A-F units.

Figure 8
Sew an A unit to 2
opposite sides of F.

12. Join four A-F units with three B-C units and two A-D units to make a row as shown in Figure 9; press. Repeat for four rows.

Figure 9
Join 4 A-F units with 3 B-C units and 2 A-D units.

13. Cut three strips red/cream plaid 6½" x 42½" along length of fabric. Join the pieced rows with the strips referring to the Placement Diagram; press seams toward strips.

14. Cut two strips red/cream plaid 8½" x 42½" along length of fabric; sew to the top and bottom of the pieced section. Press seams toward strips.

15. Cut two strips red/cream plaid 8½" x 66½" along length of fabric. Sew a strip to opposite long sides; press seams toward strips.

16. Sandwich batting between completed top and prepared backing piece; pin or baste together to hold.

17. Quilt as desired by hand or machine. When quilting is complete, remove basting or pins. Trim edges even. Bind with self-made or purchased binding to finish.

Technicolor Clamshell

BY MARGRIT HALL

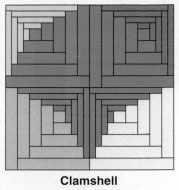

Clamshell
14" x 14" Block

When you look closely at this quilt, you see that it is actually the Log Cabin block in a new and creative shape. Each Clamshell block is made of four Log Cabin units—two with wide dark strip sections and two with narrow dark strip sections. The dark clamshell-shaped section of each block is made with the same dark print in each Log Cabin unit. The corner sections of each block use different contrasting prints depending upon what color clamshell is in the next block. No two blocks in the quilt are alike, but the technique for making each block is the same. The instructions here are for one block. Consecutive blocks are made following the color selection as show in Figure 8.

Technicolor Clamshell

Project Specifications
Quilt Size: 71" x 85"
Block Size: 14" x 14"
Number of Blocks: 20

Fabric & Batting
- 6" by fabric width strip each of 20 dark prints (D1–D20)
- 6" by fabric width strip each of 30 contrasting prints (C1–C30)
- ⅝ yard black solid
- 2½ yards border stripe
- Batting 75" x 89"
- Backing 75" x 89"
- 9¼ yards self-made or purchased binding

Supplies & Tools
- Neutral color all-purpose thread
- Variegated thread
- Basic sewing tools and supplies, rotary cutter, ruler and cutting mat

Technicolor Clamshell

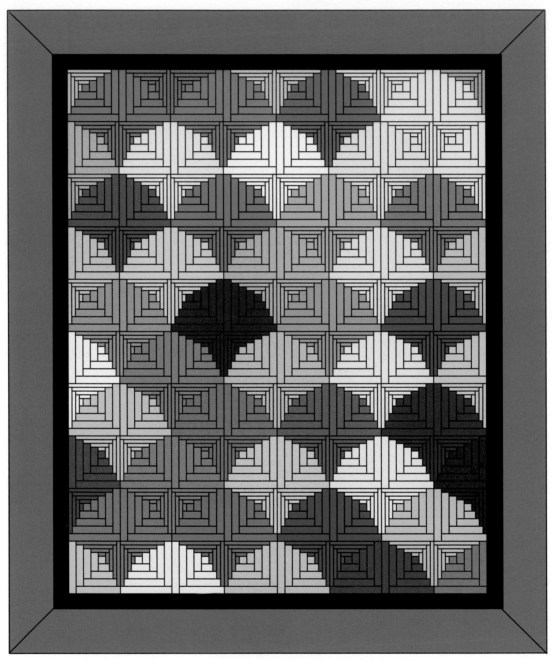

Technicolor Clamshell
Placement Diagram
71" x 85"

Instructions

1. Cut each print strip into two 1½"-wide strips and two 1"-wide strips.

2. To piece one Log Cabin unit with wide dark strip sections, place a 1" C1 strip right sides together with a 1½" D1 strip. Cut a 1½" segment from layered strips as shown in Figure 1.

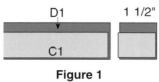

Figure 1
Cut a 1 1/2" segment
from layered strips.

3. Stitch along edge of segment; press seam toward C1 to complete unit center.

4. Place unit center right sides together with 1" C1 strip as shown in Figure 2; stitch. Trim strip even with unit center as shown in Figure 3; press seam toward strip.

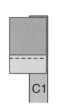

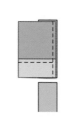

Figure 2
Place unit center
right sides
together with 1"
C1 strip.

Figure 3
Trim strip even with stitched
unit center.

5. Continue adding 1" C1 strips and 1½" D1 strips in this manner to complete one Log Cabin unit as shown in Figure 4. Press all seams away from unit center.

Figure 4
Complete 1 Log
Cabin unit as shown.

6. Repeat steps 2–5 to complete a second Log Cabin unit using 1½" D1 strips with 1" C2 strips as shown in Figure 5.

Figure 5
Complete a second Log
Cabin unit as shown.

7. To piece a Log Cabin unit with narrow dark strip sections, repeat steps 2–5 using 1½" C3 strips with 1" D1 strips as shown in Figure 6. Repeat with 1½" C4 strips and 1" D1 strips to make a second unit.

Figure 6
Piece a Log Cabin unit
with narrow dark strip
sections as shown.

Technicolor Clamshell

8. Join the four Log Cabin units with the D1 sections positioned to meet in the center to complete one Clamshell block as shown in Figure 7.

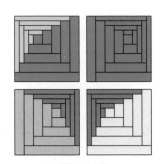

Figure 7
Join Log Cabin units to complete
1 Clamshell block.

9. Continue to piece Log Cabin units to complete 20 Clamshell blocks in print combinations as shown in Figure 8.

10. Join four blocks to make a row; repeat for five rows referring to Figure 8 for positioning of blocks.

11. Join rows to complete pieced center; press seams in one direction.

12. Cut and piece two strips each 2½" x 60 ½" and

2½" and 74½" black solid. Sew the shorter strips to the top and bottom and the longer strips to opposite sides, mitering corners. Press seams toward strips; trim excess at seam at mitered corners.

13. Cut two strips each 6" x 71½" and 6" x 85½" along length of identical sections of border stripe. Center and sew the shorter strips to the top and bottom and the longer strips to opposite sides of the pieced center; mitering corners. Press seams toward strips; trim excess at seam at mitered corners.

14. Sandwich batting between completed top and prepared backing piece; pin or baste layers together.

15. Quilt as desired by hand or machine. *Note: The quilt shown was machine-quilted using several different purchased patterns with variegated thread in the top of the machine and all-purpose thread in the bobbin.*

16. When quilting is complete, remove pins or basting; trim edges even. Bind with self-made or purchased binding to finish.

Figure 8
Piece Log Cabin units to complete 20 Clamshell blocks in print combinations shown; join blocks in rows.

Starry Night

BY KAREN NEARY

It's a summer starry night at the beach and, over the water, bursts of bright color light up the sky. You may not be at the beach to see the starry night, but this quilt will transport you there. Those tiny points in the compass stars look very difficult to piece, but they are easy if you use the paper-piecing method.

Starry Night

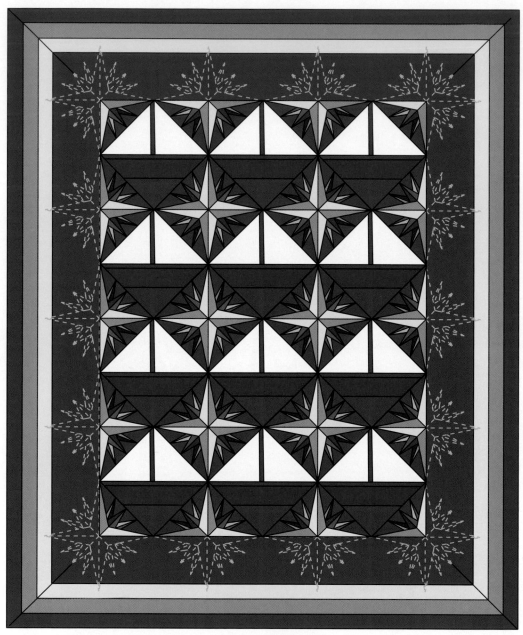

Starry Night
Placement Diagram
43 1/4" x 52 1/2"

Starry Night

Project Specifications

Quilt Size: 43¼" x 52½"

Block Size: 6½" x 6½"

Number of Blocks: 6 whole Compass, 10 half
    Compass, 4 quarter Compass and 12 Sailboats

Fabric & Batting

- ¼ yard each dark red, orange, dark orange,
  lilac and purple solids
- ⅓ yard white-on-white print
- ½ yard red solid
- 1¾ yards each gold and yellow solids
- 2 yards navy solid
- Backing 47" x 56"
- Batting 47" x 56"
- 5¾ yards self-made or purchased binding

Supplies & Tools

- Neutral color all-purpose thread
- Red and white quilting thread
- Gold metallic quilting thread
- Basic sewing supplies and tools, water-erasable
  marker or pen, paper for foundations, rotary
  cutter, ruler and cutting mat

Instructions

1. Cut two strips each navy solid along length of
fabric for borders as follows: 4½" x 48", 4½" x 57",
1¾" x 57" and 1¾" x 48". Set strips aside.

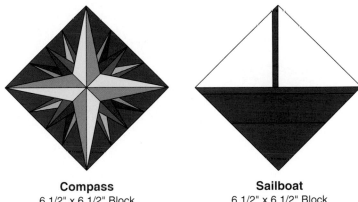

Compass
6 1/2" x 6 1/2" Block

Sailboat
6 1/2" x 6 1/2" Block

2. Cut two strips each yellow and gold solids along
length of fabric for borders as follows: 1¾" x 48" and
1¾" x 57". Set strips aside.

3. Trace patterns given for paper piecing onto foundation paper, tracing 12 sailboat patterns and 48
each right and left compass sections. Mark with
colors and numbers to indicate order of piecing.

4. Cut fabric patches at least ¼" larger than area
1 all around from navy solid. Repeat for all pieces,
cutting colors as directed on patterns.

5. Pin piece one on the unmarked side of the paper
foundation; pin piece 2 on piece 1 along edge
between pieces 1 and 2 as shown in Figure 1.

6. Turn paper to marked side; stitch on line between
pieces 1 and 2. Turn paper back over and press piece
2 flat. Continue adding pieces in numerical order.

7. When all pieces have been added, trim excess
even with outside edge of paper pattern. Do not

Starry Night

remove paper at this time. Repeat for all compass paper patterns.

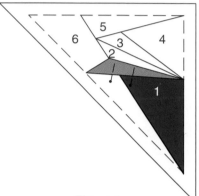

Figure 1
Pin piece 2 on piece 1 along edge between pieces 1 and 2 as shown.

Figure 2
Join a left and right compass section.

8. Join a left and right compass section as shown in Figure 2; repeat for all left and right sections. Set aside four of these units for corners.

9. Join two pieced units to make half blocks as shown in Figure 3; repeat for all units. Set aside 10 half blocks.

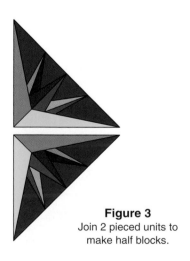

Figure 3
Join 2 pieced units to make half blocks.

10. Join remaining half blocks to complete Compass blocks; repeat for six blocks.

11. Complete 12 Sailboat blocks referring to steps 4–7.

12. Arrange corner units with half blocks and whole blocks in diagonal rows as shown in Figure 4; join in rows. Join rows to complete pieced center. Remove paper pieces.

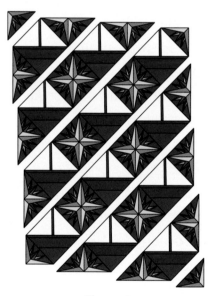

Figure 4
Arrange corner units with half blocks and whole blocks in diagonal rows as shown.

13. Sew a 4½" x 48" navy solid strip to a 1¾" x 48" yellow solid strip to a 1¾" x 48" gold solid strip to a 1¾" x 48" navy solid strip; press seams toward darker fabrics. Repeat for second 48"-long strip set and two strips sets for long sides using 57"-long strips.

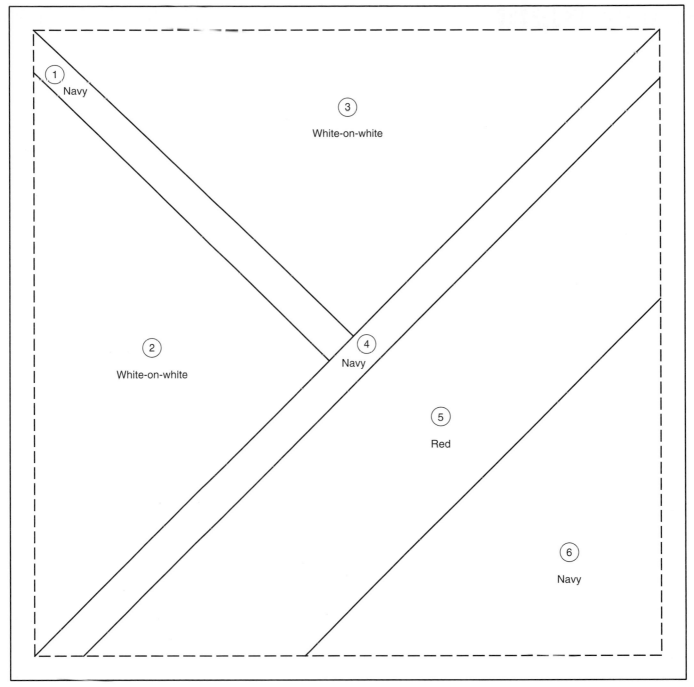

Sailboat Paper-Piecing Pattern
Make 12

14. Center and sew the longer strips to opposite long sides and shorter strips to top and bottom, matching strip seams and mitering corners. Trim excess seam allowance on wrong side to ¼" seam; press seams open.

Starry Night

15. Using the star pattern given, mark the quilting design on the wide navy solid borders referring to the Placement Diagram and using a water-erasable marker or pen.

16. Sandwich batting between completed top and prepared backing piece; pin or baste layers together to hold flat for quilting.

17. Quilt pieced area of quilt as desired by hand or machine using white and red quilting thread.

18. Using gold metallic quilting thread in the top of the machine and all-purpose thread in the bobbin, machine-quilt on marked lines for star design in border.

19. When quilting is complete, trim edges even; remove pins or basting.

20. Bind edges with self-made or purchased binding to finish.

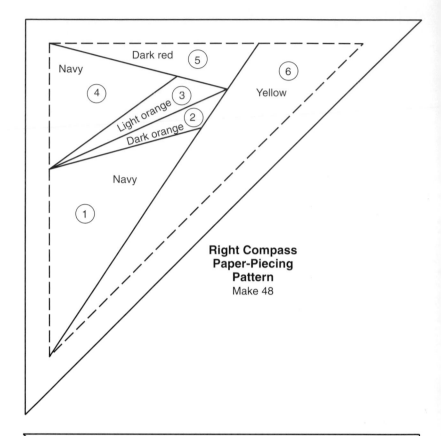

Right Compass Paper-Piecing Pattern
Make 48

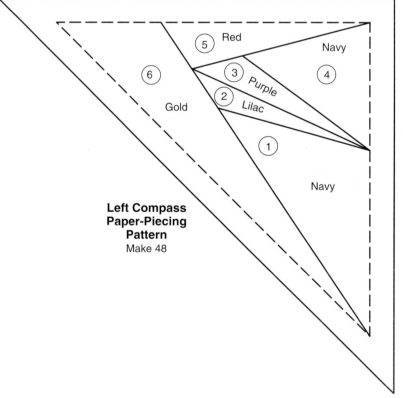

Left Compass Paper-Piecing Pattern
Make 48

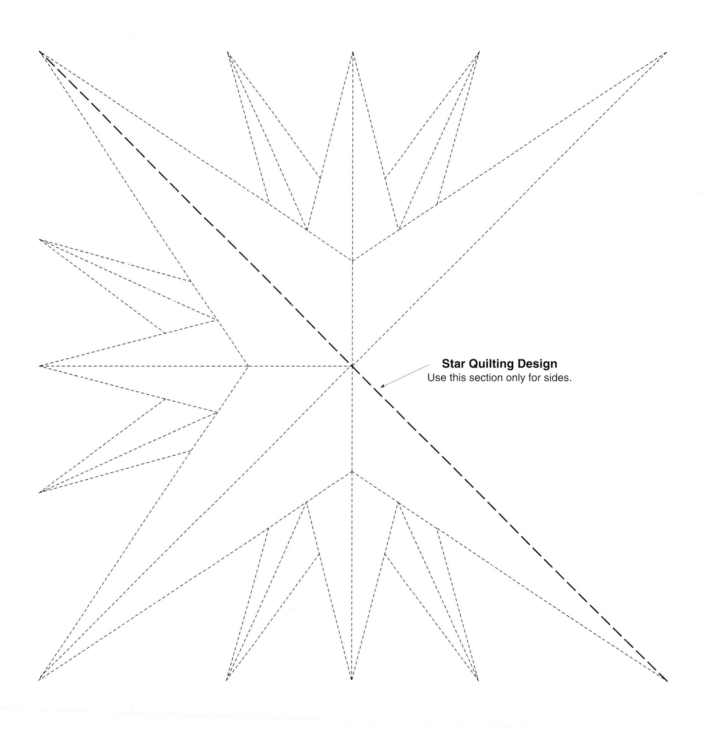

Star Quilting Design
Use this section only for sides.

Autumn Wreath

BY MARIAN SHENK

A wreath of bright-colored autumn leaves introduces the autumn quilts.

Autumn Wreath

Autumn Wreath
Placement Diagram
26" x 26"

Autumn Wreath

Project Specifications
Quilt Size: 26" x 26"

Fabric & Batting
- Scraps gold, green, tan, brown, peach and rust prints
- ⅔ yard cream-on-cream print
- Backing 30" x 30"
- Batting 30" x 30"
- 3¼ yards self-made or purchased binding

Supplies & Tools
- All-purpose thread to match fabrics
- Off-white quilting thread
- ½ yard ⅛"-wide brown bias tape
- Basic sewing tools and supplies and water-erasable marker or pencil

Instructions
1. Prepare templates using pattern pieces given. Cut as directed on each piece, adding a ⅛"–¼" seam allowance all around each appliqué piece when cutting for hand appliqué.

2. Cut a 16½" x 16½" square cream-on-cream print for background. Fold in half on both sides and crease to mark centers.

3. Copy full-size pattern onto a large piece of paper. Tape on a window. Tape background block over pattern, using center crease marks as a guide. Transfer full-size pattern onto background square using a water-erasable marker or pencil.

4. Pin pieces in place in numerical order using marked lines as a guide, overlapping as shown on pattern. Use brown bias tape for stem pieces.

5. Hand-appliqué pieces in place using all-purpose thread to match fabrics, turning under seam allowance of each piece as you stitch.

6. Sew B and BR to C as shown in Figure 1; repeat for four units. Sew a green print A to a cream-on-cream print A as shown in Figure 2; repeat for 12 A-A units.

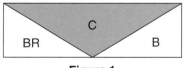

Figure 1
Sew B and BR to C.

Figure 2
Sew a green print A to a cream-on-cream print A.

7. Sew an A-A unit to each end of a B-C-BR unit as shown in Figure 3; repeat for two units. Sew a unit to opposite sides of the appliquéd center; press seams toward pieced sections.

Autumn Wreath

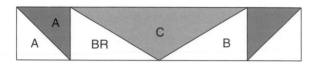

Figure 3
Sew an A-A unit to each end of a B-C-BR unit.

8. Sew two A-A units to each end of the remaining two B-C-BR units as shown in Figure 4. Sew a pieced strip to the remaining sides of the appliquéd center; press seams toward pieced sections.

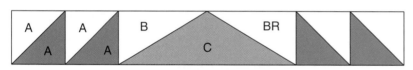

Figure 4
Sew 2 A-A units to each end of the remaining 2 B-C-BR units.

9. Cut four strips cream-on-cream print 2½" x 22½". Sew a strip to two opposite sides of the pieced and appliquéd center; press seams toward strips.

10. Sew D to each end of the remaining two strips. Sew a strip to the remaining sides of the pieced and appliquéd center; press seams toward strips.

11. Sandwich batting between completed top and prepared backing piece. Pin or baste layers together to hold flat.

12. Hand-quilt around each appliquéd shape, vein line on leaves and in the ditch of all pieced seams using off-white quilting thread.

13. Mark quilting design given on cream-on-cream print border and background corners using water-erasable marker or pencil. Hand-quilt on marked lines using off-white quilting thread.

14. When quilting is complete, trim edges even; remove pins or basting. Bind edges with self-made or purchased binding to finish. ❖

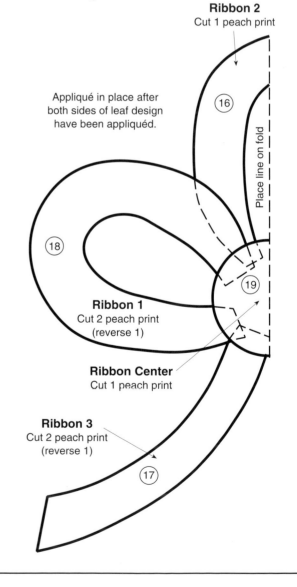

Ribbon 2
Cut 1 peach print

Appliqué in place after both sides of leaf design have been appliquéd.

16

Place line on fold

18

Ribbon 1
Cut 2 peach print
(reverse 1)

19

Ribbon Center
Cut 1 peach print

Ribbon 3
Cut 2 peach print
(reverse 1)

17

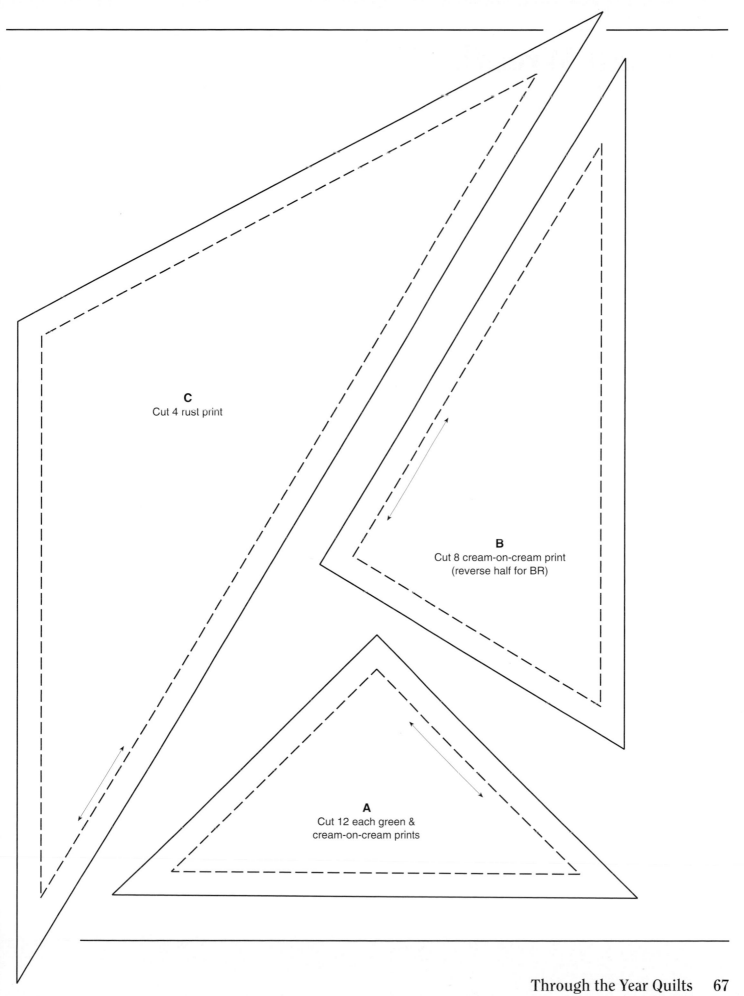

C
Cut 4 rust print

B
Cut 8 cream-on-cream print
(reverse half for BR)

A
Cut 12 each green &
cream-on-cream prints

Autumn Wreath

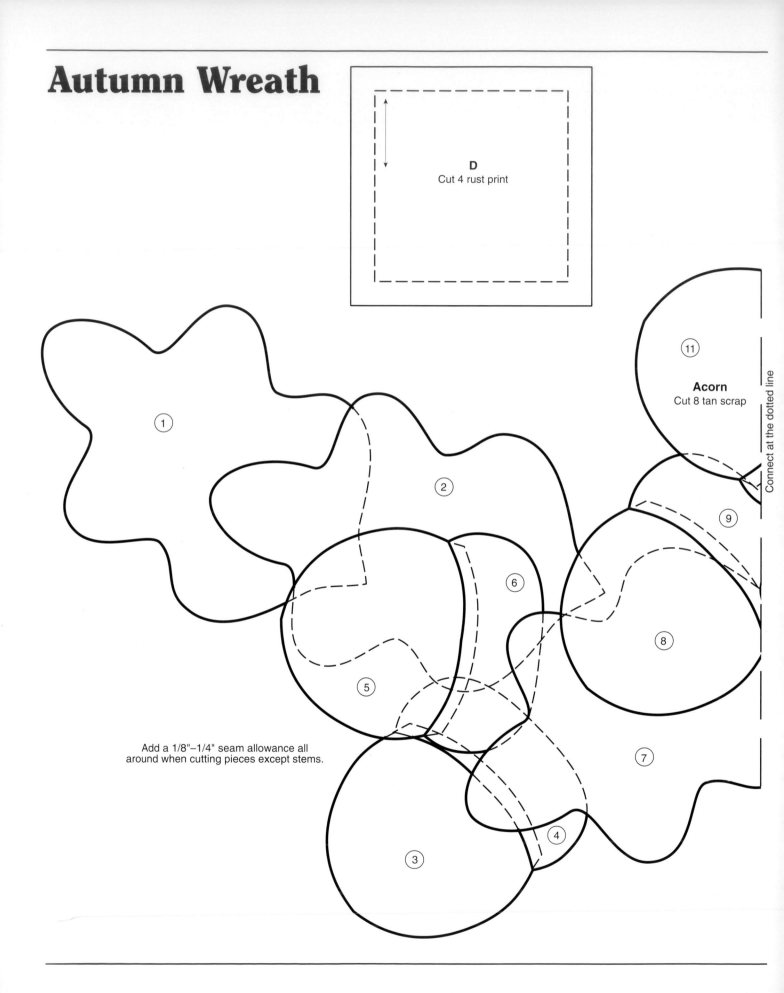

D
Cut 4 rust print

Acorn
Cut 8 tan scrap

Connect at the dotted line

Add a 1/8"–1/4" seam allowance all around when cutting pieces except stems.

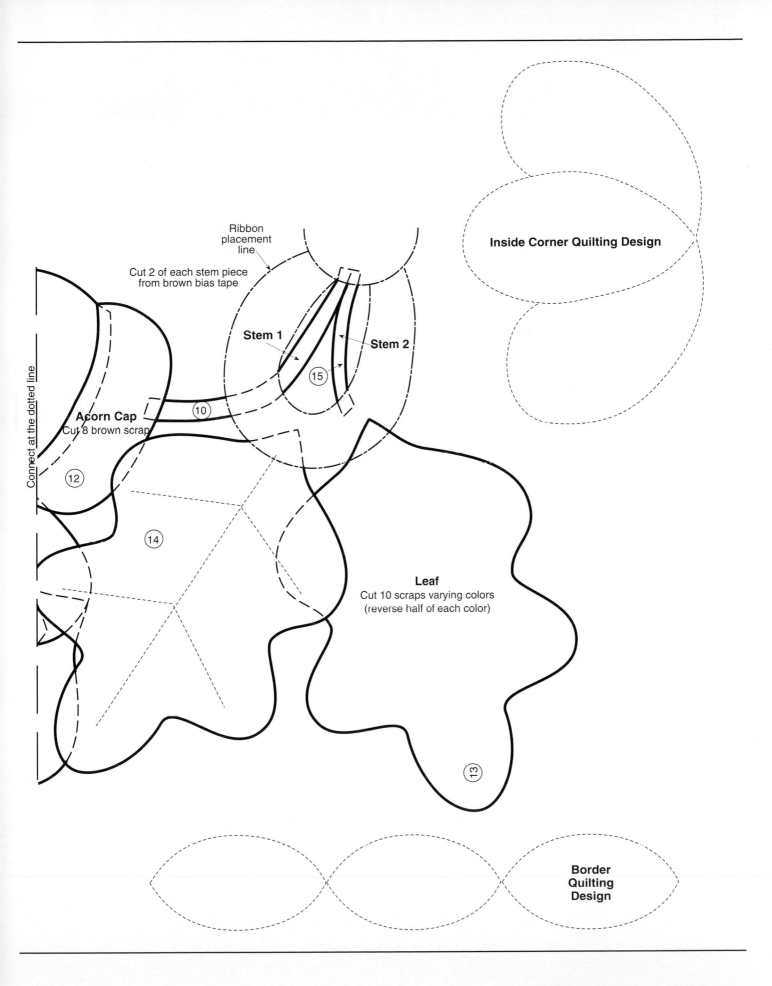

Ribbon placement line

Cut 2 of each stem piece from brown bias tape

Inside Corner Quilting Design

Connect at the dotted line

Stem 1

Stem 2

15

Acorn Cap
Cut 8 brown scrap

10

12

14

Leaf
Cut 10 scraps varying colors
(reverse half of each color)

13

**Border
Quilting
Design**

Sister's Choice

BY LUCY FAZELY

Sister's Choice
10" x 10" Block

Make this old favorite quilt with soft autumnal colors, using dark print scraps and light print scraps to create the blocks. If you like to work with templates in the traditional method of quiltmaking, the instructions are here. If you prefer to use quick-piecing techniques, you'll find those instructions here as well. Either way, you are sure to receive praise for the results.

Sister's Choice

Project Specifications

Project Size: 50" x 62"
Block Size: 10" x 10"
Number of Blocks: 12

Fabric & Batting

- ¼ yard rust print
- ⅔ yard light blue print
- Dark print scraps to total ¾ yard
- Light print scraps to total 1 yard
- 1¼ yards navy print
- Backing 54" x 66"
- Batting 54" x 66"
- 6¾ yards self-made or purchased binding

Supplies & Tools

- All-purpose thread to match fabrics
- Clear nylon monofilament
- Basic sewing tools and supplies, rotary cutter, ruler and cutting mat

Instructions

Traditional Method

1. Prepare templates using pattern pieces given; cut as directed on each piece for one block. Repeat for 12 blocks.

2. To piece one block, sew a light print B to a dark print C; repeat for four units and set aside.

Sister's Choice

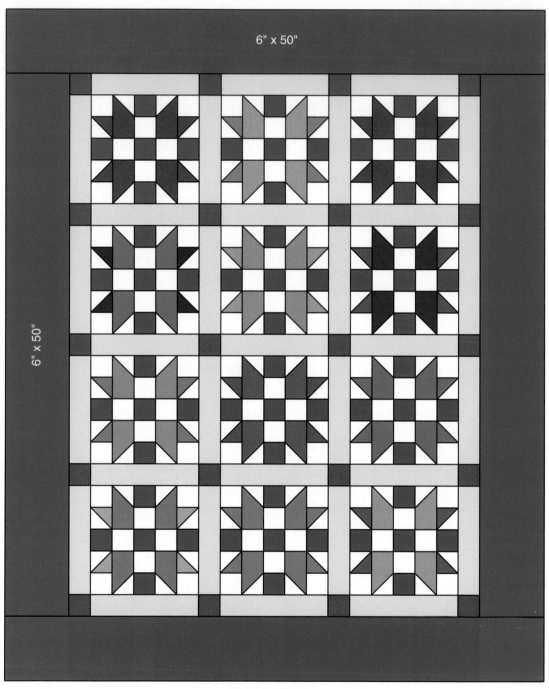

6" x 50"

6" x 50"

Sister's Choice
Placement Diagram
50" x 62"

3. Sew a light print B to a dark print B; repeat for four units and set aside.

4. Join three navy print and two light print A squares as shown in Figure 1. Join a light print and navy print A as shown in Figure 2; repeat for two units.

Figure 1
Join 3 navy print and 2
light print A squares.

Figure 2
Join a light print
and navy print A.

5. Sew a B-B unit to a light print A; sew to a B-C unit as shown in Figure 3; repeat for four units.

Figure 3
Sew a B-B unit to a light
print A; sew to a B-C unit.

6. Join two A-B-C units with an A-A unit as shown in Figure 4; repeat for two units.

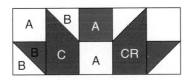

Figure 4
Join 2 A-B-C units with
an A-A unit.

7. Arrange the pieced units and join together as shown in Figure 5 to complete one block; press. Repeat for 12 blocks.

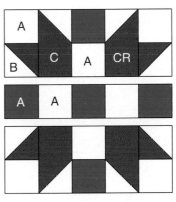

Figure 5
Arrange the pieced units and
join together as shown to
complete 1 block.

8. Cut 31 rectangles light blue print 2½" x 10½" for sashing strips. Cut 20 squares rust print 2½" x 2½" for sashing squares.

9. Join three blocks with four sashing strips to make a block row referring to Figure 6; repeat for four block rows. Press seams toward strips.

2 1/2" x 10 1/2"

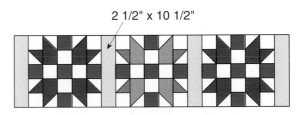

Figure 6
Join 3 blocks with 4 sashing
strips to make a block row.

10. Join three sashing strips with four sashing squares to make a sashing row as shown in Figure 7; repeat for five sashing rows. Press seams toward strips.

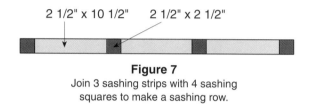

2 1/2" x 10 1/2"   2 1/2" x 2 1/2"

Figure 7
Join 3 sashing strips with 4 sashing
squares to make a sashing row.

11. Join the block rows with the sashing rows beginning and ending with a sashing row to complete the pieced center; press seams toward sashing rows.

12. Cut and piece four strips each 6½" x 50½" navy print. Sew a strip to opposite sides and then the top and bottom of the pieced center; press seams toward strips.

13. Mark a chosen quilting design on the completed quilt top. *Note: The quilt shown was machine-quilted in the ditch of seams using clear nylon monofilament in the top of the machine and all-purpose thread in the bobbin.*

14. Sandwich batting between completed top and prepared backing piece; pin or baste layers together to hold flat.

15. Quilt as desired by hand or machine. When quilting is complete, remove pins or basting; trim edges even.

16. Bind edges with self-made or purchased binding to finish.

Quicker Method

1. Cut six strips light print 2½" by fabric width. *Note: We are assuming that fabric width is 42"; if smaller strips are cut from scraps, change the number of strips to cut accordingly.* Subcut strips into 2½" square segments; you will need 96 light print squares for B.

2. Cut three strips dark print 2½" by fabric width. Subcut strips into 2½" square segments; you will need 48 dark print squares for B.

3. Cut three strips 4½" by fabric width dark print. Subcut strips into 2½" segments; you will need 48 dark print rectangles for C.

4. Cut four strips navy print and six strips light print 2½" by fabric width; subcut into 2½" square segments; you will need 60 navy print and 96 light print squares for A.

5. Cut two strips light blue print 10½" by fabric width. Subcut into 2½" segments; you will need 31 light blue print sashing strips.

6. Cut two strips rust print 2½" by fabric width. Subcut into 2½" square segments; you will need 20 rust print sashing squares.

7. Place a light print B square on a dark print C rectangle as shown in Figure 8; sew on one diagonal as shown in Figure 9.

Figure 8
Place a light print
B square on a dark
print C rectangle.

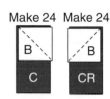

Make 24 Make 24

Figure 9
Sew on 1 diagonal.

8. Trim excess beyond seam to ¼" as shown in Figure 10; press to complete a B-C unit. Repeat for all C rectangles; set aside.

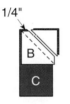

1/4"

Figure 10
Trim excess 1/4"
beyond seam.

Figure 11
Place a light print B square right
sides together with a dark print B
square; sew on 1 diagonal.

9. Place a light print B square right sides together with a dark print B square; sew on one diagonal as shown in Figure 11. Trim excess beyond seam to ¼", again referring to Figure 10; press to complete a B-B unit. Repeat for 96 B-B units.

10. Piece blocks, assemble and finish quilt as for traditional method. ❖

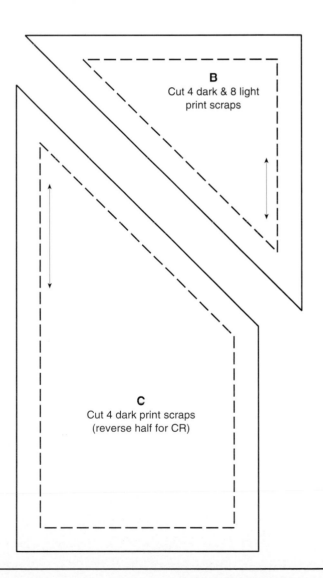

B
Cut 4 dark & 8 light
print scraps

C
Cut 4 dark print scraps
(reverse half for CR)

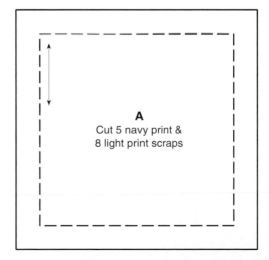

A
Cut 5 navy print &
8 light print scraps

Sunbonnet Witches

BY JUDITH SANDSTROM

Sunbonnet Witch
4 1/2" x 6 1/2" Block

It's Halloween, and good old Sunbonnet Sue has decided to join the fun. She's exchanged her sweet little sunbonnet for a witch's hat, and she's ready to trick or treat. Perhaps she thinks no one will recognize her, but we quiltmakers are not deceived!

Sunbonnet Witches

Project Specifications

Quilt Size: 20½" x 26½"

Block Size: 4½" x 6½"

Number of Blocks: 9

Fabric & Batting

- 9 scraps black prints or plaids 3" x 4" for dresses
- 3" x 5" scrap black dot for cats
- 10" x 10" scrap black solid for hats and shoes
- 6" x 6" scrap orange print for pumpkins
- 4" x 4" scrap green print for stems
- ¼ yard black print for border
- ¼ yard dark green print for border and sashing
- ⅜ yard cream-on-cream print
- Backing 24" x 30"
- Lightweight batting 24" x 30"
- 3 yards self-made or purchased binding

Supplies & Tools

- 1 spool each black, green and orange all-purpose thread
- ½ yard fusible transfer web
- Basic sewing tools and supplies

Instructions

1. Prewash and iron all fabrics.

2. Cut nine cream-on-cream print rectangles 5" x 7".

3. Cut four strips dark green print 1" by fabric width. Cut these strips to make six 7", four 15" and two 22" strips.

4. Place each pattern piece right side down on the paper side of the fusible transfer web; trace around shapes as directed on pattern, tracing all pieces of the same color together. Cut paper sections apart

Sunbonnet Witches

2 1/2" x 20 1/2"

2 1/2" x 21 1/2"

1/2" x 21 1/2"

Sunbonnet Witch
Placement Diagram
20 1/2" x 26 1/2"

and fuse to the wrong side of the appropriate fabrics as directed on pattern pieces.

5. Cut out shapes on traced lines; remove paper backing.

6. Center a dress, with hat, shoes, pumpkin and stem on each cream-on-cream print rectangle, overlapping pieces in numerical order as marked on patterns. Fuse in place following manufacturer's instructions; repeat for nine blocks.

7. Using thread to match fabrics, machine-appliqué pieces in place.

8. Join three blocks with two 1" x 7" dark green print sashing strips to make a row as shown in Figure 1; press seams toward strips. Repeat for three rows with blocks with cats in different location on each row referring to the Placement Diagram.

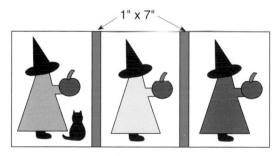

Figure 1
Join blocks with 1" x 7" sashing strips.

9. Join the rows with four 1" x 15" sashing strips beginning and ending with a strip as shown in Figure 2; press seams toward strips. Sew a 1" x 22" strip to each long side; press seams toward strips.

Figure 2
Join rows with 1" x 15" sashing strips.

10. Cut two strips each black print 3" x 22" and 3" x 20½". Sew the longer strips to opposite sides and the shorter strips to the top and bottom; press seams toward strips.

11. Sandwich batting between completed top and prepared backing piece. Pin or baste layers together to hold flat.

Sunbonnet Witches

12. Quilt as desired by hand or machine. When quilting is complete, remove pins or basting. Trim edges even.

13. Bind with self-made or purchased binding to finish. ❖

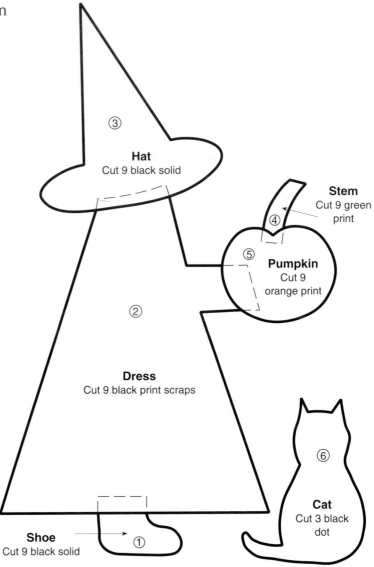

Hat
Cut 9 black solid

Stem
Cut 9 green print

Pumpkin
Cut 9 orange print

Dress
Cut 9 black print scraps

Cat
Cut 3 black dot

Shoe
Cut 9 black solid

Maple Leaf Harvest

BY LISA CHRISTENSEN

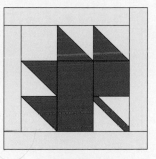

Maple Leaf A
8" x 8" Block
Make 29

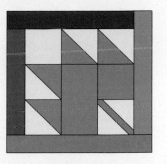

Maple Leaf B
8" x 8" Block
Make 30

A quilt that truly says autumn, this quilt uses assorted leaf-colored fabrics to create the leaves falling across the quilt. This is another quilt that answers the needs of those fabric collectors who always seem to have small scraps of fabric available. If you prefer, you can purchase fabric just for this quilt and make all of your maple leaves in the same color.

Maple Leaf Harvest

Project Specifications

Quilt Size: 76⅞" x 99⅝"

Block Size: 8" x 8"

Number of Blocks: 59

Fabric & Batting

- 9 yards total assorted autumn leaf-color fabrics
- 5 yards total assorted light prints
- Backing 81" x 104"
- Batting 81" x 104"
- 10½ yards self-made or purchased binding

Supplies & Tools

- Neutral color all-purpose thread
- Quilting thread
- Basic sewing supplies and tools, ruler, rotary cutter and cutting mat

Instructions

1. For each leaf shape, cut the following from the same autumn leaf-colored fabric: two 2½" x 2½" squares for A; one 2½" x 4½" rectangle for B; and two 2⅞" x 2⅞" squares each cut on one diagonal to make C triangles.

2. For background for each block, cut the following from the same light print fabric: one 2½" x 2½" square for A; one 2¼" x 2¼" square cut on one diagonal to make D triangles; and two 2⅞" x 2⅞" squares each cut on one diagonal to make C triangles.

3. For border strips for each block cut light print to match background for Maple Leaf A blocks or four different dark prints for Maple Leaf B blocks as follows: one 1½" x 6½" for E; two 1½" x 7½" for F; and one 1½" x 8½" for G.

Maple Leaf Harvest

4. To piece one block, sew an autumn leaf-colored C triangle to a light print C triangle; repeat for four C-C units.

5. Place a D triangle on an autumn leaf-colored A square as shown in Figure 1; sew on the diagonal of D. Trim seam to ¼"; press D triangle flat as shown in Figure 2.

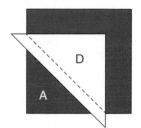

Figure 1
Place a D triangle on an autumn leaf-colored A square; stitch on the diagonal.

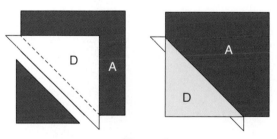

Figure 2
Trim seam to 1/4"; press D triangle flat.

6. Place the second D triangle on the A-D unit as shown in Figure 3; stitch, trim and press as in step 5 to complete a stem unit as shown in Figure 4.

7. Referring to Figure 5, join two C-C units with A; join two C-C units with B; and sew A to the A-D stem unit.

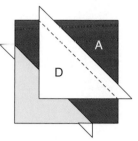

Figure 3
Place the second D triangle on the A square as shown.

Figure 4
The stitched stem unit is shown.

8. Join the pieced units as shown in Figure 6 to complete leaf portion of block.

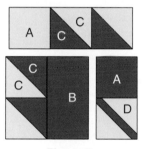

Figure 5
Join pieces as shown.

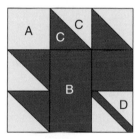

Figure 6
Join the pieced units to complete leaf portion of block.

9. Sew background E, F and G pieces to sides of block referring to Figure 7 to complete one Maple Leaf A block; repeat for 29 blocks.

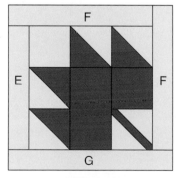

Figure 7
Sew background E, F and G pieces to sides of block to complete 1 Maple Leaf A block.

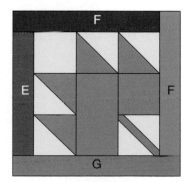

Figure 8
Sew the 4 different dark print E, F and G pieces to sides of block to complete 1 Maple Leaf B block.

Maple Leaf Harvest

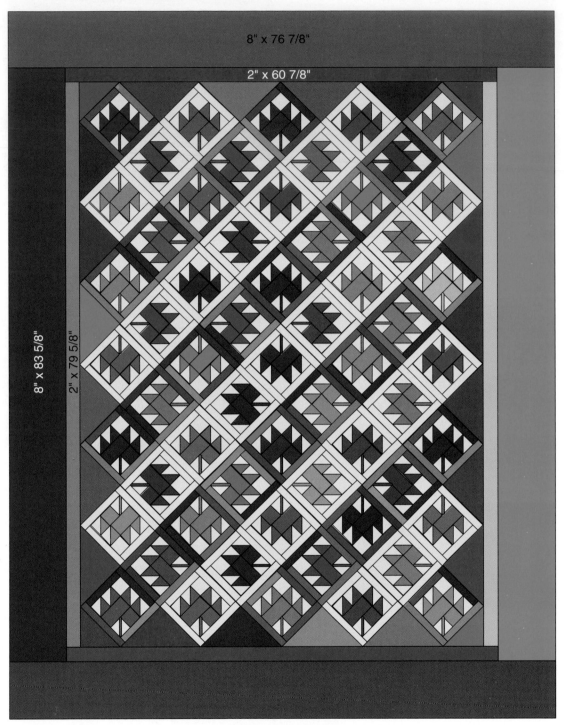

8" x 76 7/8"

2" x 60 7/8"

8" x 83 5/8"

2" x 79 5/8"

Maple Leaf Harvest
Placement Diagram
76 7/8" x 99 5/8"

10. Sew the four different dark print E, F and G pieces to sides of block referring to Figure 8 to complete one Maple Leaf B block; repeat for 30 blocks.

11. Cut one square each of five different autumn leaf-colored prints 12⅝" x 12⅝". Cut each square in half on both diagonals to make H triangles as shown in Figure 9. You will need 20 H triangles.

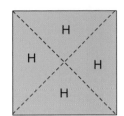

Figure 9
Cut 12 5/8" x 12 5/8" square
in half on both diagonals to
make H triangles.

12. Cut one each of two different autumn leaf-colored prints 6½" x 6½"; cut each square in half on one diagonal to make I triangles. You will need four I triangles.

13. Arrange blocks with H and I triangles in diagonal rows, keeping Maple Leaf A blocks in rows together and Maple Leaf B blocks in rows together referring to Figure 10. Join blocks in rows; join rows to complete pieced center.

14. Cut and piece two strips each from four different autumn leaf-colored prints 2½" x 61⅜" and 2½" x 80⅛". Sew the longer strips to opposite long sides and shorter strips to the top and bottom; press seams toward strips.

15. Cut and piece two strips each from four different autumn leaf-colored prints 8½" x 77⅜" and 8½" x 84⅛". Sew the longer strips to opposite long sides and shorter strips to the top and bottom; press seams toward strips.

Figure 10
Arrange A and B blocks in diagonal rows with H and I triangles.

16. Sandwich batting between completed top and prepared backing; pin or baste layers together to hold flat.

17. Quilt as desired by hand or machine. *Note: The quilt shown was machine-quilted on the diagonal with lines 1¼" apart through all blocks and a meandering design in H and I triangles and on border corners. Border strips were quilted in straight lines 2" apart across width. Clear nylon monofilament was used in the top of the machine and all-purpose thread to match backing in the bobbin.*

18. When quilting is complete, trim edges even. Bind with self-made or purchased binding to finish. ❖

Winter Wreath

BY MARIAN SHENK

Holly leaves and berries make the perfect decorations for a winter wreath that introduces our winter quilts.

Winter Wreath

2" x 22"

F

Winter Wreath
Placement Diagram
26" x 26"

Winter Wreath

Project Specifications

Quilt Size: 26" x 26"

Fabric & Batting

- Scraps gold-on-green and red-and-green prints, red/green plaid, green metallic dot and green metallic speckled
- ½ yard red metallic speckled
- ¾ yard cream-on-cream print
- Backing 30" x 30"
- Batting 30" x 30"
- 3¼ yards self-made or purchased binding

Supplies & Tools

- All-purpose thread to match fabrics
- Off-white quilting thread
- Basic sewing tools and supplies and water-erasable marker or pencil

Instructions

1. Prepare templates using pattern pieces given. Cut as directed on each piece, adding a ⅛"–¼" seam allowance all around each appliqué piece when cutting for hand appliqué.

2. Cut a 16½" x 16½" square cream-on-cream print for background. Fold in half on both sides and crease to mark centers.

3. Copy full-size pattern onto a large piece of paper. Tape on a window. Tape background block over pattern, using center crease marks as a guide. Transfer full-size pattern onto background square using a water-erasable marker or pencil.

4. Pin pieces in place in numerical order using marked lines as a guide, overlapping as shown on pattern.

5. Hand-appliqué pieces in place using all-purpose thread to match fabrics.

6. Sew A to two adjacent sides of B as shown in Figure 1. Sew A-B to adjacent sides of C as shown in Figure 2; add D and DR, again referring to Figure 2. Repeat for four units.

Figure 1
Sew A to 2 adjacent
sides of B.

Figure 2
Sew A-B to adjacent sides
of C; add D and DR.

7. Sew a red metallic speckled E to a cream-on-cream print E as shown in Figure 3; repeat for 12 E-E units. Sew an E-E unit to each end of an A-B-C-D unit as shown in Figure 4. Sew a unit to opposite sides of the appliquéd center; press seams toward pieced sections.

Winter Wreath

Figure 3
Sew a red E
to a cream E.

Figure 4
Sew an E-E unit to each end of an A-B-C-D unit.

8. Sew an E-E unit to each end of the remaining two pieced strips as shown in Figure 5. Sew a pieced strip to the remaining sides of the appliquéd center; press seams toward pieced sections.

Figure 5
Sew an E-E unit to each end of the remaining 2 pieced strips.

9. Cut four strips cream-on-cream print 2½" x 22½". Sew a strip to two opposite sides of the pieced and appliquéd center; press seams toward strips.

10. Sew F to each end of the remaining two strips. Sew a strip to the remaining sides of the pieced and appliquéd center; press seams toward strips.

11. Sandwich batting between completed top and prepared backing piece. Pin or baste layers together to hold flat.

12. Hand-quilt around each appliquéd shape, vein line on leaves and in the ditch of all pieced seams using off-white quilting thread.

13. Mark quilting designs given on cream-on-cream print border, in wreath center and on background corners using water-erasable marker or pencil. Hand-quilt on marked lines using off-white quilting thread.

14. When quilting is complete, trim edges even; remove pins or basting. Bind edges with self-made or purchased binding to finish. ❖

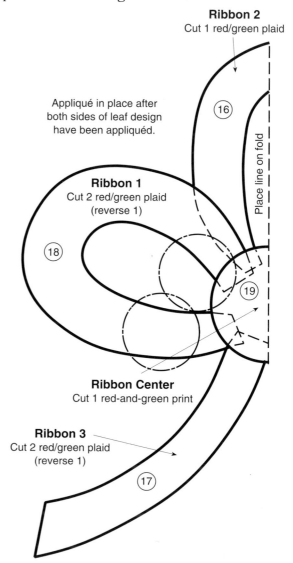

Ribbon 2
Cut 1 red/green plaid

Appliqué in place after
both sides of leaf design
have been appliquéd.

Ribbon 1
Cut 2 red/green plaid
(reverse 1)

Place line on fold

Ribbon Center
Cut 1 red-and-green print

Ribbon 3
Cut 2 red/green plaid
(reverse 1)

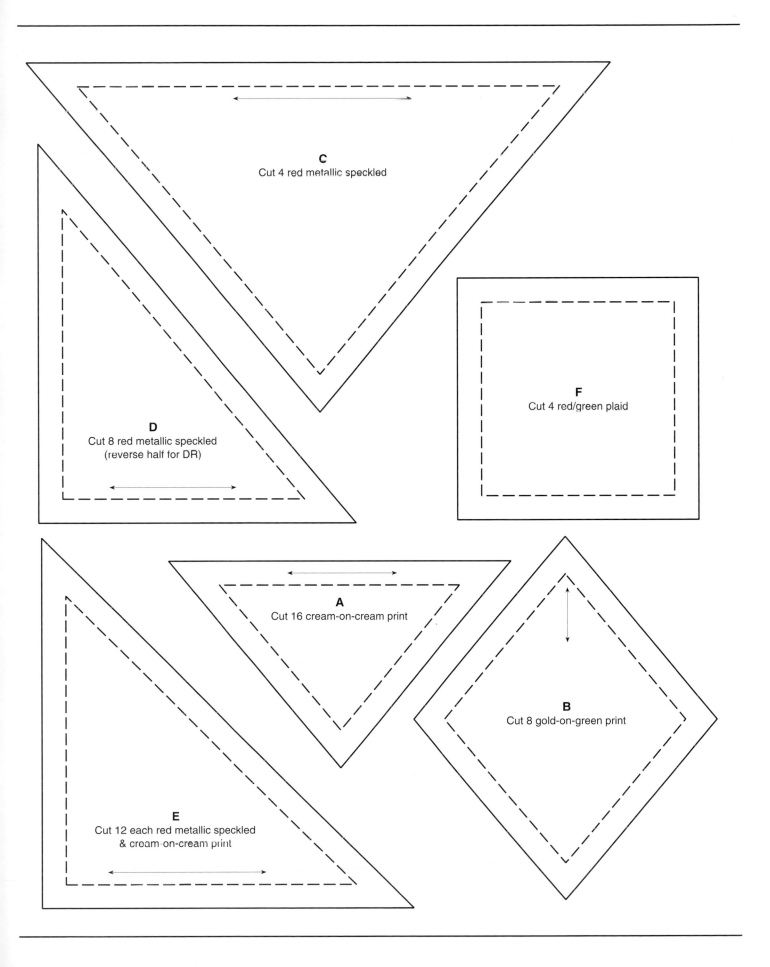

C
Cut 4 red metallic speckled

D
Cut 8 red metallic speckled
(reverse half for DR)

F
Cut 4 red/green plaid

A
Cut 16 cream-on-cream print

B
Cut 8 gold-on-green print

E
Cut 12 each red metallic speckled
& cream-on-cream print

Winter Wreath

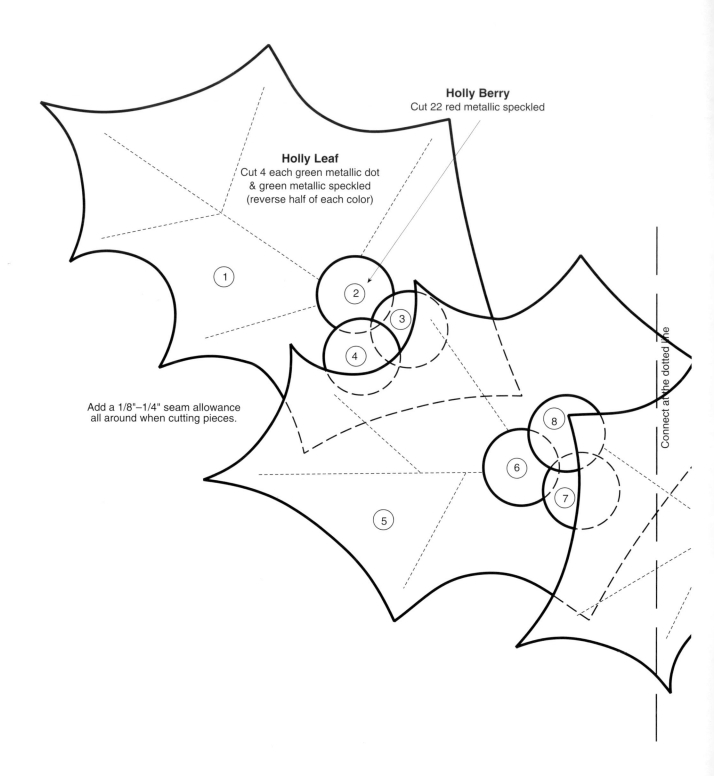

Holly Berry
Cut 22 red metallic speckled

Holly Leaf
Cut 4 each green metallic dot
& green metallic speckled
(reverse half of each color)

Add a 1/8"–1/4" seam allowance
all around when cutting pieces.

Connect at the dotted line

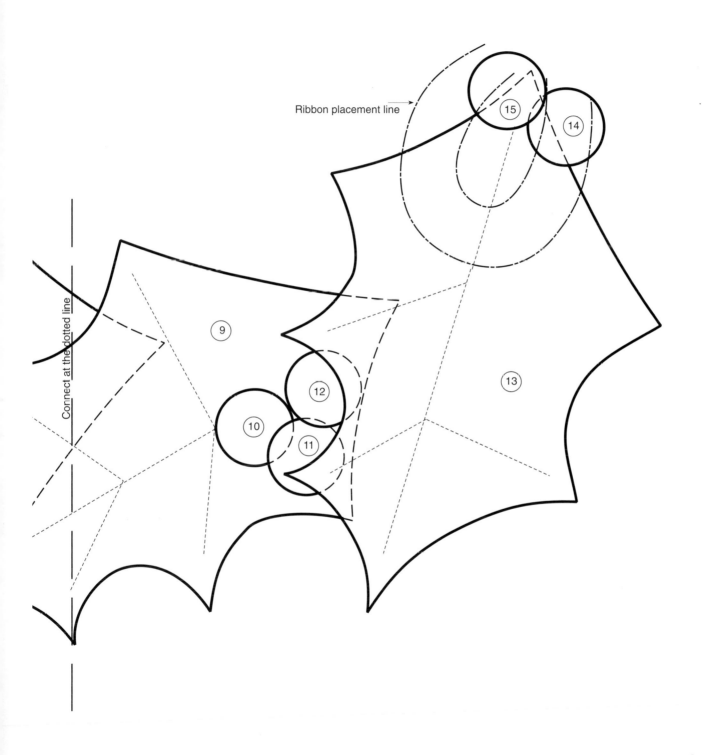

Ribbon placement line

Connect at the dotted line

⑨ ⑩ ⑪ ⑫ ⑬ ⑭ ⑮

Winter Wreath

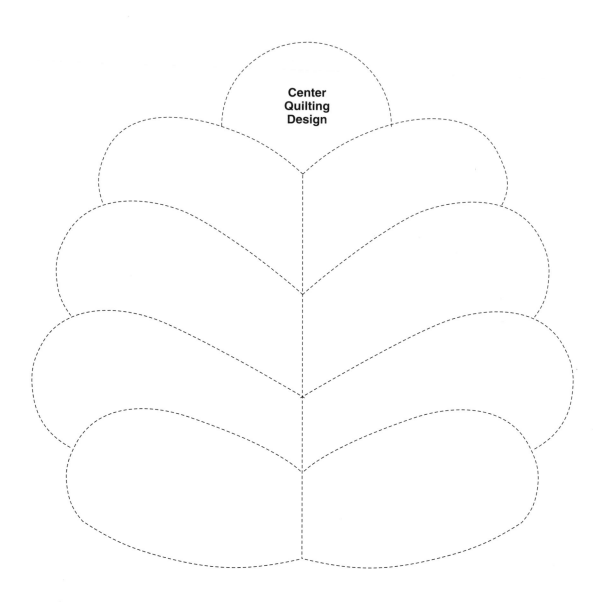

Center
Quilting
Design

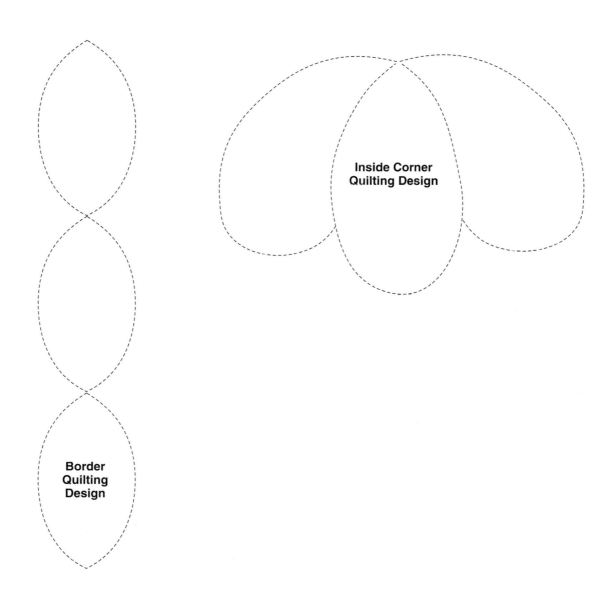

Inside Corner Quilting Design

Border Quilting Design

Winter Bears Quilt

BY LISA CHRISTENSEN

If you are a teddy bear lover—or know someone who is—this is the quilt for you! Four adorable bears, each made from a different brown/black fabric, sit in the center of the quilt, surrounded by stars and evergreen trees. The instructions may look complicated, but the entire quilt is actually easy to construct because it is made entirely of squares and rectangles.

Winter Bears Quilt

4 1/2" x 42"

1 1/2" x 33"

4 1/2" x 45"

1 1/2" x 42"

Winter Bears Quilt
Placement Diagram
42" x 54"

Winter Bears Quilt

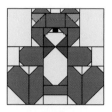

Bear
10" x 10" Block
Make 4

Tree
5" x 6" Block
Make 8

Star
5" x 5" Block
Make 16

Project Specifications

Quilt Size: 42" x 54"

Star Block Size: 5" x 5"

Tree Block Size: 5" x 6"

Bear Block Size: 10" x 10"

Number of Star Blocks: 16

Number of Tree Blocks: 8

Number of Bear Blocks: 4

Fabric & Batting

- 4 assorted fat quarters brown/black prints for bears and tree trunks
- 9" x 11" piece tan check for inside ears
- 9" x 11" piece black print for nose
- 1 fat quarter tan-on-tan print for muzzle and chest
- 4 assorted fat eighths burgundy prints for stars and bow ties
- 4 assorted fat eighths blue prints for stars
- 4 assorted fat eighths green prints for trees
- 2 yards tan mottled for background
- 1¼ yards winter print for borders and binding
- Backing 46" x 58"
- Batting 46" x 58"

Supplies & Tools

- Neutral color all-purpose thread
- 1 spool clear nylon monofilament
- Basic sewing tools and supplies

Instructions

1. Cut fabrics as directed in the Cutting Chart on page 101.

2. Place a smaller piece on a larger piece with right sides together as shown in Figure 1. Stitch as shown by dotted lines on drawing. Trim ¼" beyond stitched line to reduce bulk if desired as shown in Figure 2.

Figure 1
Place a smaller piece on a larger with pieces right sides together as shown.

1/4"

Figure 2
Trim 1/4" beyond stitched line to reduce bulk.

3. Press piece to right side as shown in Figure 3. Continue adding pieces referring to figure drawings given for each block, checking the colored section given with each step to show which part of the block is being pieced as shown in Figure 4.

Figure 3
Press piece to right side as shown.

Figure 4
The colored section shows the stitched unit.

Winter Bears Quilt

4. Construct four Bear blocks (one from each brown/black print and one bow tie from each burgundy print), eight Tree blocks (two from each green print) and 16 Star blocks (two from each burgundy and blue print).

5. Cut the following from background fabric: four 5½" x 5½" squares; four 4" x 6½" rectangles; and two 3½" x 6½" rectangles.

6. Join three Star blocks with a 5½" x 5½" back-ground square referring to Figure 5 for positioning of pieced blocks with the square. Repeat for four units.

7. Join the background rectangles with four Tree blocks, again referring to Figure 5 for positioning of rectangles; press seams in one direction.

8. Join Bear blocks with Star units to make rows, again referring to Figure 5; press seams in one direction.

9. Join rows to complete pieced center; press seams in one direction.

10. Cut two strips each background fabric 2" x 42½" and 2" x 33½". Sew the longer strips to opposite long sides and shorter strips to the top and bottom; press seams toward strips.

11. Cut and piece two strips each winter print 5" x 42½" and 5" x 45½". Sew the longer strips to opposite long sides and shorter strips to the top and bottom; press seams toward strips.

Figure 5
Join squares and rectangles with pieced blocks as shown.

Cutting Chart

Star Fabric (from each)	
16 squares	1½" x 1½"
2 squares	2½" x 2½"
Bear Fabric (from each)	
4 squares	1½" x 1½"
1 rectangle	1½" x 3"
2 squares	2" x 2"
2 rectangles	1" x 2½"
2 rectangles	1¾" x 2½"
1 rectangle	2" x 2½"
2 rectangles	2½" x 3"
2 rectangles	2" x 4½"
2 rectangles	2¾" x 4½"
Nose Fabric	
1 strip	1" x 6"
Bow Tie Fabric (from each)	
4 squares	1¾" x 1¾"
Inside Ear Fabric	
8 squares	2" x 2"

Muzzle & Chest Fabric	
2 strips	1½" x 6"
4 rectangles	2" x 3"
4 rectangles	3" x 4½"
Tree Fabric (from each)	
2 rectangles	2" x 3½"
2 rectangles	2" x 4½"
2 rectangles	2" x 5½"
Tree Trunk Fabric (from each)	
2 rectangles	1½" x 2"
Background	
32 squares	1" x 1"
8 squares	1¼" x 1¼"
4 rectangles	1" x 1½"
40 squares	1½" x 1½"
4 rectangles	1½" x 3"
8 rectangles	1¾" x 2½"
8 squares	2½" x 2½"
8 rectangles	3" x 4½"
16 rectangles	1" x 2"
16 rectangles	1½" x 2"
112 squares	2" x 2"
80 rectangles	2" x 2½"

12. Sandwich batting between completed top and prepared backing piece; pin or baste layers together to hold flat.

13. Quilt as desired by hand or machine. When quilting is complete, remove pins or basting; trim edges even.

14. Prepare 5¾ yards 2½"-wide binding from winter print. Bind edges, mitering corners and overlapping ends. ❖

Winter Bears Quilt

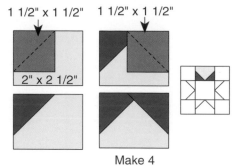

1 1/2" x 1 1/2"   1 1/2" x 1 1/2"

2" x 2 1/2"

Make 4

Figure 6	
To make 1 Star block:	
Fabric	**Pieces**
Star	8—1 1/2" x 1 1/2"
	1—2 1/2" x 2 1/2"
Background	4—2" x 2"
	4—2" x 2 1/2"

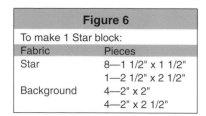

2" x 2"   2" x 2"

Make 2

Combine units to complete 1 Star block.

2 1/2" x 2 1/2"

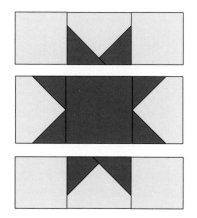

Figure 7	
To make 1 Bear block:	
Fabric	**Pieces**
Bear	2—1" x 2 1/2"
	2—2" x 2"
	1—2" x 2 1/2"
	4—1 1/2" x 1 1/2"
	2—1 3/4" x 2 1/2"
	2—2 1/2" x 3"
	2—2" x 4 1/2"
	2—2 3/4" x 4 1/2"
	1—1 1/2" x 3"
Inside Ear	2—2" x 2"
Nose	1—1" x 6"
Muzzle	2—1 1/2" x 6"
	1—2" x 3"
Bow Tie	4—1 3/4" x 1 3/4"
Chest	1—3" x 4 1/2"
Background	8—1" x 1"
	1—1" x 1 1/2"
	10—1 1/2" x 1 1/2"
	2—1 3/4" x 2 1/2"
	2—1 1/4" x 1 1/4"
	2—2 1/2" x 2 1/2"
	1—1 1/2" x 3"
	2—3" x 4 1/2"

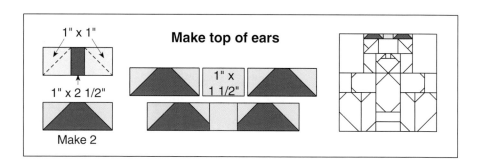

1" x 1"

Make top of ears

1" x 1 1/2"

1" x 2 1/2"

Make 2

Make ears

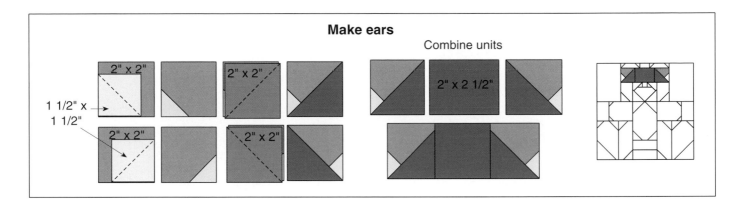

Combine units

1 1/2" x 1 1/2"

2" x 2"

2" x 2"

2" x 2 1/2"

Make nose

1 1/2" x 6"

1" x 6"

1 1/2" x 6"

Cut 4 units 1" wide. This makes noses for all 4 bears.

1"

Combine units

2" x 3"

Nose unit

Assemble head

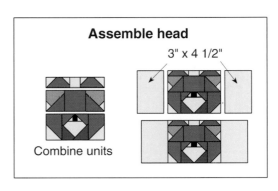

3" x 4 1/2"

Combine units

Make face

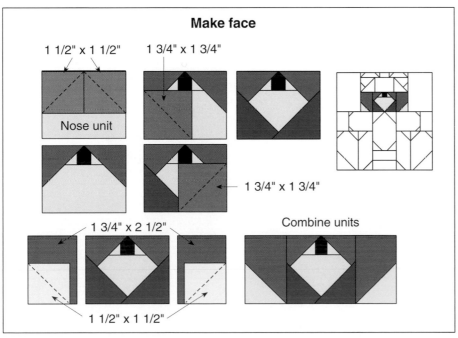

1 1/2" x 1 1/2"

1 3/4" x 1 3/4"

Nose unit

1 3/4" x 1 3/4"

1 3/4" x 2 1/2"

Combine units

1 1/2" x 1 1/2"

Winter Bears Quilt

Make arms

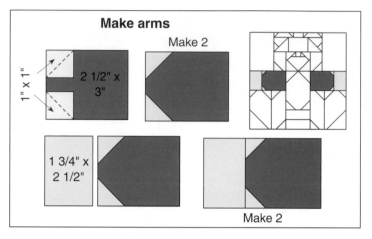

Make 2

1" x 1"

2 1/2" x 3"

1 3/4" x 2 1/2"

Make 2

Make feet

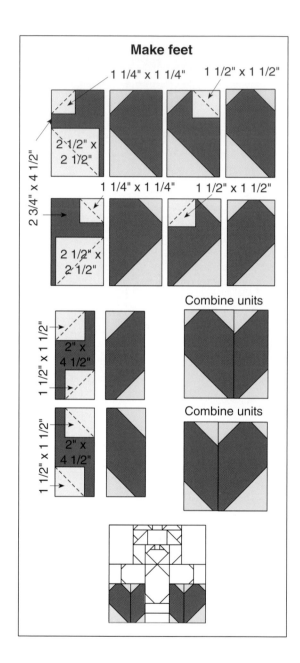

1 1/4" x 1 1/4"   1 1/2" x 1 1/2"

2 1/2" x 2 1/2"

2 3/4" x 4 1/2"

1 1/4" x 1 1/4"   1 1/2" x 1 1/2"

2 1/2" x 2 1/2"

Combine units

1 1/2" x 1 1/2"

2" x 4 1/2"

Combine units

1 1/2" x 1 1/2"

2" x 4 1/2"

Make chest

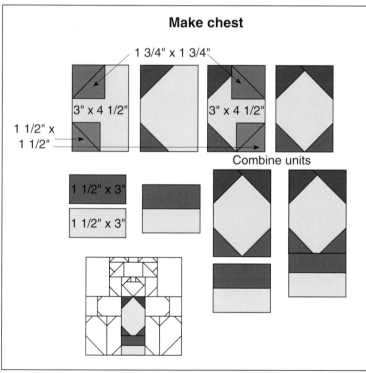

1 3/4" x 1 3/4"

3" x 4 1/2"

3" x 4 1/2"

1 1/2" x 1 1/2"

Combine units

1 1/2" x 3"

1 1/2" x 3"

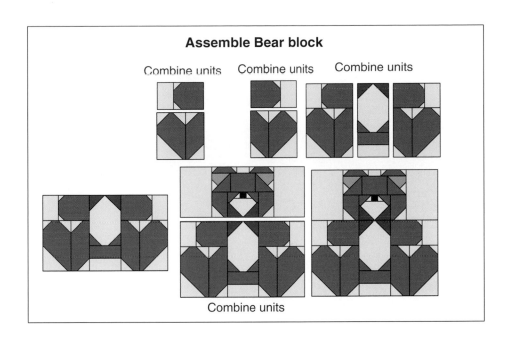

Assemble Bear block

Combine units Combine units Combine units

Combine units

Figure 8	
To make 1 Tree block:	
Fabric	**Pieces**
Tree	1 2" x 3 1/2"
	1 2" x 4 1/2"
	1 2" x 5 1/2"
Trunk	1 1 1/2" x 2"
Background	2 1 1/2" x 2"
	2 1" x 2"
	6 2" x 2"
	2 2" x 2 1/2"

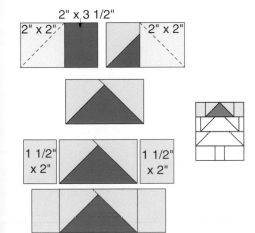

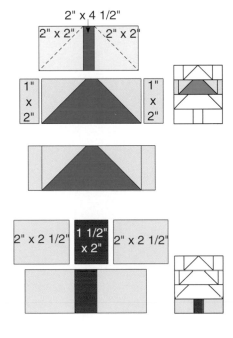

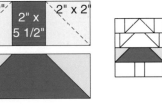

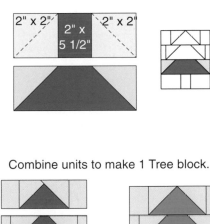

Combine units to make 1 Tree block.

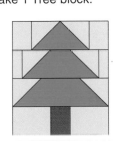

Stars of Hope

BY LUCY FAZELY

Star of Hope
16" x 16" Block

While not strictly a Christmas quilt, the choice of burgundy fabrics and the green holly print give this quilt a holiday feel. It's the perfect quilt to sleep under while you are waiting for Santa Claus. With our quickpiecing construction methods the quilt could be ready for Christmas. If you don't want a Christmas quilt, choosing other fabric could change the character of your quilt.

Stars of Hope

Project Specifications
Quilt Size: 44" x 60"
Block Size: 16" x 16"
Number of Blocks: 6

Fabric & Batting
- ½ yard small burgundy print
- ¾ yard green holly print
- 1 yard large burgundy print
- 2 yards cream print
- Backing 48" x 64"
- Batting 48" x 64"
- 6¼ yards self-made or purchased binding

Supplies & Tools
- Neutral color all-purpose thread
- Clear nylon monofilament
- Basic sewing tools and supplies, rotary cutter, ruler and cutting mat

Instructions
1. Cut 17 strips cream print and nine strips green holly print 2½" by fabric width; subcut strips into 2½" square segments for A. You will need 264 cream print and 144 green holly print A squares.

2. Cut four strips cream print 4½" by fabric width; subcut strips into 4½" square segments for B. You will need 30 B squares.

Stars of Hope

6" x 44"

6" x 48"

Stars of Hope
Placement Diagram
44" x 60"

3. Cut three strips small burgundy print 4½" by fabric width; subcut into 2½" segments for C. You will need 48 C rectangles.

4. Set aside 24 cream print A squares. Draw a diagonal line on the wrong side of the remaining 240 squares.

5. Place a marked A square right sides together with each green holly print A square; stitch on marked line. Trim seam to ¼" beyond seam as shown in Figure 1. Press seams toward darker fabric.

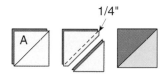

Figure 1
Place a marked A square right sides together with a green holly print A square; stitch on marked line. Trim seam to 1/4" beyond seam line as shown.

6. Repeat step 5 using two marked A squares with each C rectangle as shown in Figure 2.

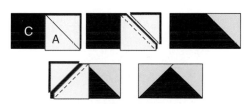

Figure 2
Place a marked A square right sides together with a C rectangle; stitch on marked line. Trim seam to 1/4" beyond seam line; repeat on the opposite end as shown.

7. Join two A-C units as shown in Figure 3; repeat for 24 units.

Figure 3
Join 2 A-C units as shown.

8. Arrange the A-C units in rows with the cream print B squares as shown in Figure 4; join the units in rows. Join the rows to complete one center block unit; repeat for six units.

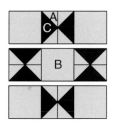

Figure 4
Arrange the A-C units in rows with the cream print B squares as shown.

9. Join six cream/green A units to make a border unit as shown in Figure 5; repeat for 24 units.

Figure 5
Join 6 cream/green A units to make a border unit.

Stars of Hope

10. Sew a border unit to opposite sides of the pieced center block unit as shown in Figure 6; repeat for six units.

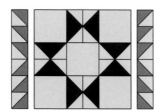

Figure 6
Sew a border unit to
opposite sides of the
pieced center block unit.

11. Sew a cream print A square to each end of the remaining border units. Sew these units to the pieced center block units to complete the six blocks as shown in Figure 7.

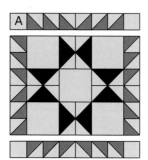

Figure 7
Join units to
complete 1 block.

12. Join two blocks to make a row; repeat for three rows. Join the block rows to complete the pieced center.

13. Cut (and piece) two strips each large burgundy print 6½" x 44½" and 6½" x 48½". Sew the longer strips to opposite long sides and the shorter strips to the top and bottom of the pieced center; press seams toward strips.

14. Sandwich batting between completed top and prepared backing; pin or baste layers in place to hold flat.

15. Quilt as desired by hand or machine. *Note: The quilt shown was machine-quilted in the ditch of seam using clear nylon monofilament in the top of the machine and all-purpose thread in the bobbin.*

16. When quilting is complete, trim edges even; remove pins or basting.

17. Bind edges with self-made or purchased binding to finish. ❖

Snowman Wall Quilt

BY KAREN NEARY

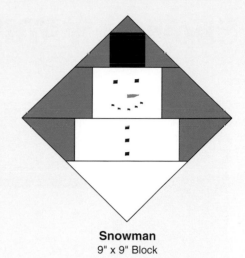

Snowman
9" x 9" Block

Most snowman quilt designs are appliquéd. This pieced design, therefore, will please quilters who prefer piecing to appliqué. The snowmen are pieced very quickly, and their faces are machine embroidered. The entire quilt, which can be assembled in a few hours, is sure to please everyone.

Snowman Wall Quilt

Project Specifications

Quilt Size: 25½" x 25½"

Block Size: 9" x 9"

Number of Blocks: 5

Fabric & Batting

- ½ yard white-on-white print
- 1 yard blue snowflake print
- 6" x 9" rectangle black satin
- Backing 29" x 29"
- Batting 29" x 29"
- 3 yards self-made or purchased white binding
- All-purpose thread to match fabrics
- Black and orange rayon thread
- ½ yard tear-off fabric stabilizer
- Basic sewing tools and supplies, rotary cutter, ruler and cutting mat

Instructions

1. Prepare templates using pattern pieces given. Cut as directed on each piece for one block; repeat for five blocks.

2. To piece one block, sew F to D to F; add E.

3. Sew G to C to GR. Sew H to B to HR; add A.

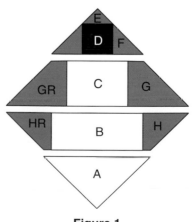

Figure 1
Join the pieced units as
shown to complete 1 block.

Snowman Wall Quilt

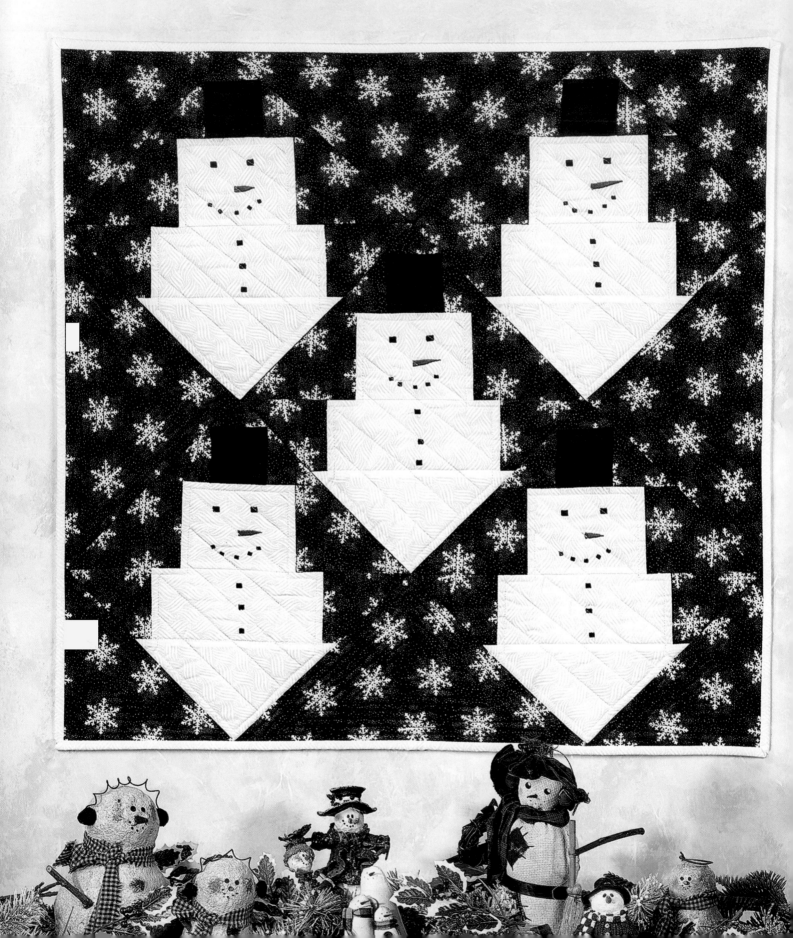

4. Join the pieced units as shown in Figure 1 to complete one block; repeat for five blocks and press.

5. Cut five 5" x 7" pieces tear-off fabric stabilizer. Pin behind each pieced block.

6. Using black rayon thread in the top of the machine and all-purpose thread in the bobbin, satin-stitch eye, mouth and button squares referring to lines marked on pattern pieces for placement. Repeat with orange rayon thread to stitch the nose. Remove tear-off fabric stabilizer when stitching is complete.

7. Cut one 14" x 14" square blue snowflake print. Cut the square in half on both diagonals as shown in Figure 2 to make side fill-in triangles.

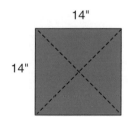

Figure 2
Cut the 14" x 14" square in half on both diagonals to make side fill-in triangles.

8. Cut two 7¼" x 7 ¼" squares blue snowflake print. Cut each square in half on one diagonal to make corner triangles.

9. Arrange blocks and triangles in diagonal rows referring to Figure 3. Join pieces and blocks in diagonal rows; join rows and add the two corner triangles to complete the pieced top.

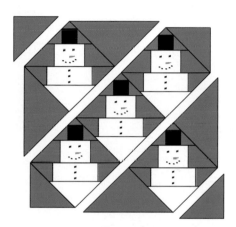

Figure 3
Arrange blocks and triangles in diagonal rows.

10. Sandwich batting between completed top and prepared backing piece; pin or baste layers together to hold flat.

11. Quilt as desired by hand or machine. *Note: The quilt shown was machine-quilted using white thread on the snowman designs in diagonal lines and blue thread on the background in lines ¼" apart echoing the triangle shapes.*

12. When quilting is complete, trim edges even and remove pins or basting.

13. Bind edges with self-made or purchased white binding to finish. ❖

Snowman Wall Quilt

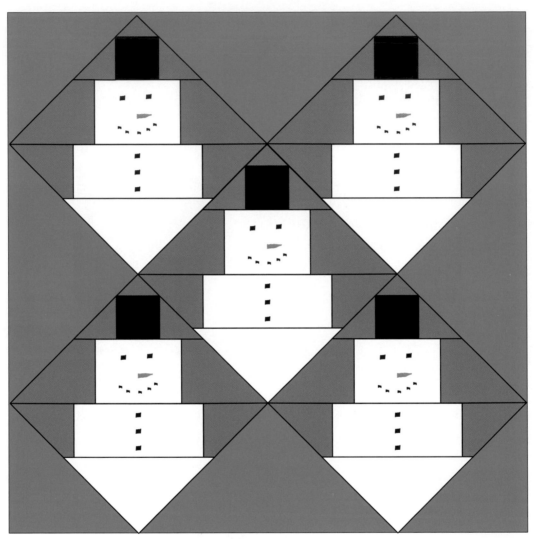

Snowman Wall Quilt
Placement Diagram
25 1/2" x 25 1/2"

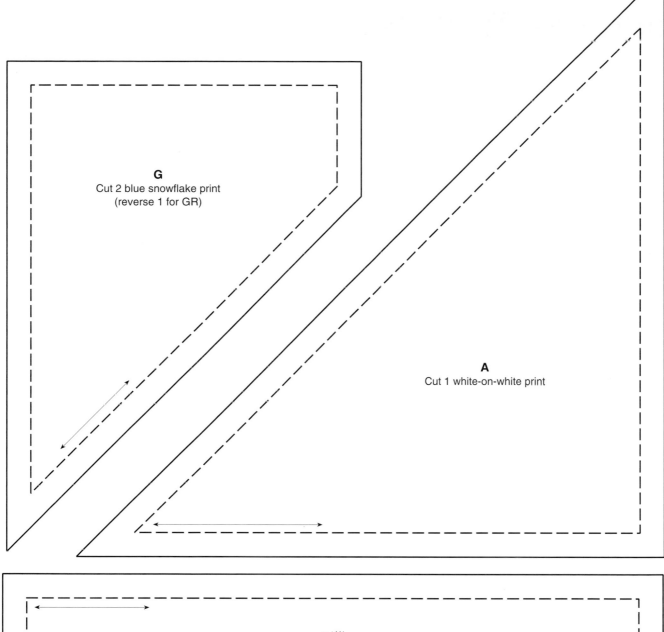

G
Cut 2 blue snowflake print
(reverse 1 for GR)

A
Cut 1 white-on-white print

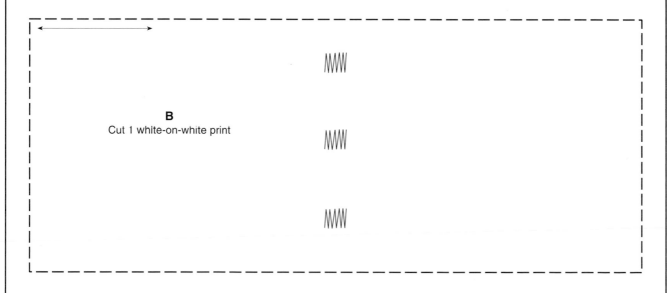

B
Cut 1 white-on-white print

Snowman Wall Quilt

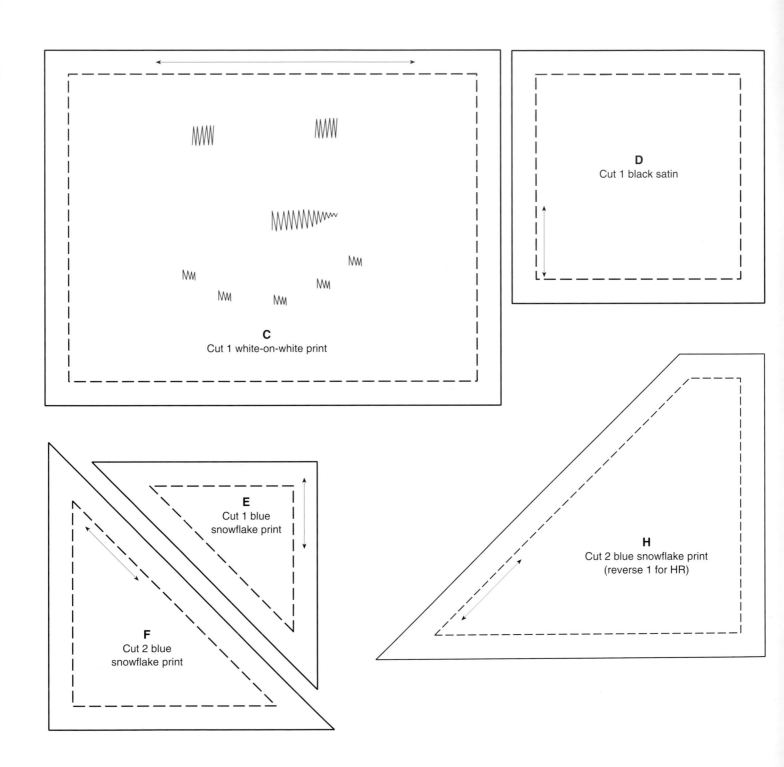

C
Cut 1 white-on-white print

D
Cut 1 black satin

E
Cut 1 blue
snowflake print

F
Cut 2 blue
snowflake print

H
Cut 2 blue snowflake print
(reverse 1 for HR)

General Instructions

Quiltmaking Basics

Materials & Supplies

Fabrics
Fabric Choices. Quilts and quilted projects combine fabrics of many types. Use same-fiber-content fabrics when making quilted items, if possible.

Buying Fabrics. One hundred percent cotton fabrics are recommended for making quilts. Choose colors similar to those used in the quilts shown or colors of your own preference. Most quilt designs depend more on contrast of values than on the colors used to create the design.

Preparing the Fabric for Use. Fabrics may be prewashed depending on your preference. Whether you prewash or not, be sure your fabrics are colorfast and won't run onto each other when washed after use.

Fabric Grain. Fabrics are woven with threads going in a crosswise and lengthwise direction. The threads cross at right angles—the more threads per inch, the stronger the fabric.

The crosswise threads will stretch a little. The lengthwise threads will not stretch at all. Cutting the fabric at a 45-degree angle to the crosswise and lengthwise threads produces a bias edge which stretches a great deal when pulled (Figure 1).

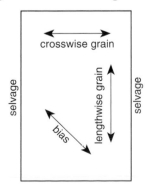

Figure 1
Drawing shows lengthwise, crosswise and bias threads.

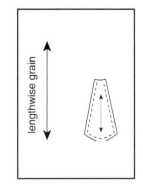

Figure 2
Place the template with marked arrow on the lengthwise grain of the fabric.

If templates are given with patterns in this book, pay careful attention to the grain lines marked with arrows. These arrows indicate that the piece should be placed on the lengthwise grain with the arrow running on one thread. Although it is not necessary to examine the fabric and find a thread to match to, it is important to try to place the arrow with the lengthwise grain of the fabric (Figure 2).

Thread
For most piecing, good-quality cotton or cotton-covered polyester is the thread of choice. Inexpensive polyester threads are not recommended because they can cut the fibers of cotton fabrics.

Choose a color thread that will match or blend with the fabrics in your quilt. For projects pieced with dark and light color fabrics choose a neutral thread color, such as a medium gray, as a compromise between colors. Test by pulling a sample seam.

Batting
Batting is the material used to give a quilt loft or thickness. It also adds warmth.

Batting size is listed in inches for each pattern to reflect the size needed to complete the quilt according to the instructions. Purchase the size large enough to cut the size you need for the quilt of your choice.

Some qualities to look for in batting are drapability, resistance to fiber migration, loft and softness.

Tools & Equipment
There are few truly essential tools and little equipment required for quiltmaking. Basics include needles (hand-sewing and quilting betweens), pins (long, thin, sharp pins are best), sharp scissors or shears, a thimble, template materials (plastic or cardboard), marking tools (chalk marker, water-erasable pen and a No. 2 pencil are a few) and a quilting frame or hoop. For piecing and/or quilting by machine, add a sewing machine to the list.

Other sewing basics such as a seam ripper, pincushion, measuring tape and an iron are also necessary. For choosing colors

General Instructions

or quilting designs for your quilt, or for designing your own quilt, it is helpful to have on hand graph paper, tracing paper, colored pencils or markers and a ruler.

For making strip-pieced quilts, a rotary cutter, mat and specialty rulers are often used. We recommend an ergonomic rotary cutter, a large self-healing mat and several rulers. If you can choose only one size, a 6" x 24" marked in ⅛" or ¼" increments is recommended.

Construction Methods

Traditional Templates. While some quilt instructions in this book use rotary-cut strips and quick sewing methods, many patterns require a template. Templates are like the pattern pieces used to sew a garment. They are used to cut the fabric pieces that make up the quilt top. There are two types—templates that include a ¼" seam allowance and those that don't.

Choose the template material and the pattern. Transfer the pattern shapes to the template material with a sharp No. 2 lead pencil. Write the pattern name, piece letter or number, grain line and number to cut for one block or whole quilt on each piece as shown in Figure 3.

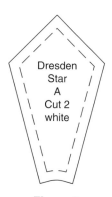

Figure 3
Mark each template with the pattern name and piece identification.

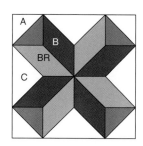

Figure 4
This pattern uses reversed pieces.

Some patterns require a reversed piece (Figure 4). These patterns are labeled with an R after the piece letter; for example, B and BR. To reverse a template, first cut it with the labeled side up and then with the labeled side down. Compare these to the right and left fronts of a blouse. When making a garment, you accomplish reversed pieces when cutting the pattern on two

layers of fabric placed with right sides together. This can be done when cutting templates as well.

If cutting one layer of fabric at a time, first trace the template onto the backside of the fabric with the marked side down; turn the template over with the marked side up to make reverse pieces.

Hand-Piecing Basics. When hand-piecing it is easier to begin with templates that do not include the ¼" seam allowance. Place the template on the wrong side of the fabric, lining up the marked grain line with lengthwise or crosswise fabric grain. If the piece does not have to be reversed, place with labeled side up. Trace around shape; move, leaving ½" between the shapes, and mark again.

When you have marked the appropriate number of pieces, cut out pieces, leaving ¼" beyond marked line all around each piece.

To join two units, place the patches with right sides together. Stick a pin in at the beginning of the seam through both fabric patches, matching the beginning points (Figure 5); for hand-piecing, the seam begins on the traced line, not at the edge of the fabric (see Figure 6).

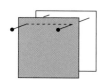

Figure 5
Stick a pin through fabrics to match the beginning of the seam.

Figure 6
Begin hand-piecing at seam, not at the edge of the fabric. Continue stitching along seam line.

Thread a sharp needle; knot one strand of the thread at the end. Remove the pin and insert the needle in the hole; make a short stitch and then a backstitch right over the first stitch. Continue making short stitches with several stitches on the needle at one time. As you stitch, check the back piece often to assure accurate stitching on the seam line. Take a stitch at the end of the seam; backstitch and knot at the same time as shown in Figure 7. Seams on hand-pieced fabric patches may be finger-pressed toward the darker fabric.

To sew units together, pin fabric patches together, matching seams. Sew as above except where seams meet; at these

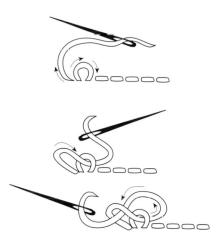

Figure 7
Make a loop in backstitch to make a knot.

intersections, backstitch, go through seam to next piece and backstitch again to secure seam joint.

Not all pieced blocks can be stitched with straight seams or in rows. Some patterns require set-in pieces. To begin a set-in seam, pin one side of the square to the proper side of the star point with right sides together, matching corners. Start stitching at the seam line on the outside point; stitch on the marked seam line to the end of the seam line at the center referring to Figure 8.

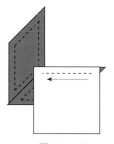

Figure 8
To set a square into a diamond point, match seams and stitch from outside edge to center.

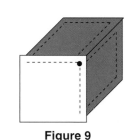

Figure 9
Continue stitching the adjacent side of the square to the next diamond shape in 1 seam from center to outside as shown.

Bring around the adjacent side and pin to the next star point, matching seams. Continue the stitching line from the adjacent seam through corners and to the outside edge of the square as shown in Figure 9.

Machine-Piecing. If making templates, include the ¼" seam allowance on the template for machine-piecing. Place template

on the wrong side of the fabric as for hand-piecing except butt pieces against one another when tracing.

Set machine on 2.5 or 12–15 stitches per inch. Join pieces as for hand-piecing for set-in seams; but for other straight seams, begin and end sewing at the end of the fabric patch sewn as shown in Figure 10. No backstitching is necessary when machine-stitching.

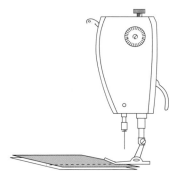

Figure 10
Begin machine-piecing at the end of the piece, not at the end of the seam.

Join units as for hand-piecing referring to the piecing diagrams where needed.

Chain piecing (Figure 11— sewing several like units before sewing other units) saves time by eliminating beginning and ending stitches.

Figure 11
Units may be chain-pieced to save time.

When joining machine-pieced units, match seams against each other with seam allowances pressed in opposite directions to reduce bulk and make perfect matching of seams possible (Figure 12).

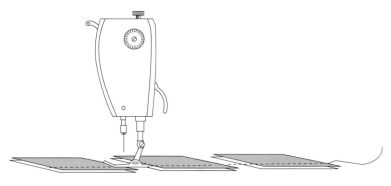

Figure 12
Sew machine-pieced units with seams pressed in opposite directions.

Quick-Cutting. Templates can be completely eliminated when using a rotary cutter with a plastic ruler and mat to cut fabric strips.

General Instructions

When rotary-cutting strips, straighten raw edges of fabric by folding fabric in fourths across the width as shown in Figure 13. Press down flat; place ruler on fabric square with edge of fabric and make one cut from the folded edge to the outside edge. If strips are not straightened, a wavy strip will result as shown in Figure 14.

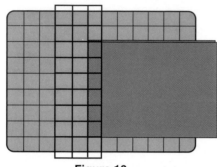

Figure 13
Fold fabric and straighten as shown.

Figure 14
Wavy strips result if fabric is not straightened before cutting.

Always cut away from your body, holding the ruler firmly with the non-cutting hand. Keep fingers away from the edge of the ruler as it is easy for the rotary cutter to slip and jump over the edge of the ruler if cutting is not properly done.

If a square is required for the pattern, it can be subcut from a strip as shown in Figure 15.

Figure 15
If cutting squares, cut proper-width strip into same-width segments. Here, a 2" strip is cut into 2" segments to create 2" squares. These squares finish at 1 1/2" when sewn.

If you need right triangles with the straight grain on the short sides, you can use the same method, but you need to figure out how wide to cut the strip. Measure the finished size of one short side of the triangle. Add ⅞" to this size for seam allowance. Cut fabric strips this width; cut the strips into the same increment to create squares. Cut the squares on the diagonal to produce triangles. For example, if you need a triangle with a 2" finished height, cut the strips 2⅞" by the width of the

fabric. Cut the strips into 2⅞" squares. Cut each square on the diagonal to produce the correct-size triangle with the grain on the short sides (Figure 16).

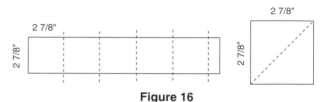

Figure 16
Cut 2" (finished size) triangles from 2 7/8" squares as shown.

Triangles sewn together to make squares are called half-square triangles or triangle/squares. When joined, the triangle/square unit has the straight of grain on all outside edges of the block.

Another method of making triangle/squares is shown in Figure 17. Layer two squares with right sides together; draw a diagonal line through the center. Stitch ¼" on both sides of the line. Cut apart on the drawn line to reveal two stitched triangle/squares.

Figure 17
Mark a diagonal line on the square; stitch 1/4" on each side of the line. Cut on line to reveal stitched triangle/squares.

If you need triangles with the straight of grain on the diagonal, such as for fill-in triangles on the outside edges of a diagonal-set quilt, the procedure is a bit different.

To make these triangles, a square is cut on both diagonals; thus, the straight of grain is on the longest or diagonal side (Figure 18). To figure out the size to cut the square, add 1¼" to the needed finished size of the longest side of the triangle. For example, if you need a triangle with a 12" finished diagonal, cut a 13¼" square.

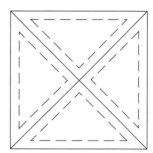

Figure 18
Add 1 1/4" to the finished size of the longest side of the triangle needed and cut on both diagonals to make a quarter-square triangle.

If templates are given, use their measurments to cut fabric strips to correspond with that measurement. The template may be used on the strip to cut pieces quickly. Strip cutting works best for squares, triangles, rectangles and diamonds. Odd-shaped templates are difficult to cut in multiple layers or using a rotary cutter.

Quick-Piecing Method. Lay pieces to be joined under the presser foot of the sewing machine right sides together. Sew an exact ¼" seam allowance to the end of the piece; place another unit right next to the first one and continue sewing, adding a piece after every stitched piece, until all of the pieces are used up (Figure 19).

Figure 19
Sew pieces together in a chain.

When sewing is finished, cut threads joining the pieces apart. Press seam toward the darker fabric.

Appliqué

Appliqué. Appliqué is the process of applying one piece of fabric on top of another for decorative or functional purposes.

Making Templates. Most appliqué designs given here are shown as full-size drawings for the completed designs. The drawings show dotted lines to indicate where one piece overlaps another. Other marks indicate placement of embroidery stitches for decorative purposes such as eyes, lips, flowers, etc.

For hand appliqué, trace each template onto the right side of the fabric with template right side up. Cut around shape, adding a ⅛"–¼" seam allowance.

Before the actual appliqué process begins, cut the background block. If you have a full-size drawing of the design, it might help you to draw on the background block to help with placement.

Transfer the design to a large piece of tracing paper. Place the paper on top of the design; use masking tape to hold in place. Trace design onto paper.

If you don't have a light box, tape the pattern on a window; center the background block on top and tape in place. Trace the design onto the background block with a water-erasable

marker or light lead or chalk pencil. This drawing will mark exactly where the fabric pieces should be placed on the background block.

Hand Appliqué. Traditional hand appliqué uses a template made from the desired finished shape without seam allowance added.

After fabric is prepared, trace the desired shape onto the right side of the fabric with a water-erasable marker or light lead or chalk pencil. Leave at least ½" between design motifs when tracing to allow for the seam allowance when cutting out the shapes.

When the desired number of shapes needed has been drawn on the fabric pieces, cut out shapes leaving ⅛"–¼" all around drawn line for turning under.

Turn the shape's edges over on the drawn or stitched line. When turning in concave curves, clip to seams and baste the seam allowance over as shown in Figure 20.

Figure 20
Concave curves should
be clipped before turning
as shown.

During the actual appliqué process, you may be layering one shape on top of another. Where two fabrics overlap, the underneath piece does not have to be turned under or stitched down.

If possible, trim away the underneath fabric when the block is finished by carefully cutting away the background from underneath and then cutting away unnecessary layers to reduce bulk and avoid shadows from darker fabrics showing through on light fabrics.

For hand appliqué, position the fabric shapes on the background block and pin or baste them in place. Using a blind stitch or appliqué stitch, sew pieces in place with matching thread and small stitches. Start with background pieces first and work up to foreground pieces. Appliqué the pieces in place on the background in numerical order, if given, layering as necessary.

Machine Appliqué. There are several products available to help make the machine-appliqué process easier and faster.

Fusible transfer web is a commercial product similar to iron-on interfacings except it has two sticky sides. It is used to

General Instructions

adhere appliqué shapes to the background with heat. Paper is adhered to one side of the web.

To use, reverse pattern and draw shapes onto the paper side of the web; cut, leaving a margin around each shape. Place on the wrong side of the chosen fabric; fuse in place referring to the manufacturer's instructions. Cut out shapes on the drawn line. Peel off the paper and fuse in place on the background fabric. Transfer any detail lines to the fabric shapes. This process adds a little bulk or stiffness to the appliquéd shape and makes hand-quilting through the layers difficult.

For successful machine appliqué a tear-off stabilizer is recommended. This product is placed under the background fabric while machine appliqué is being done. It is torn away when the work is finished. This kind of stabilizer keeps the background fabric from pulling during the machine-appliqué process.

During the actual machine-appliqué process, you will be layering one shape on top of another. Where two fabrics overlap, the underneath piece does not have to be turned under or stitched down.

Thread the top of the machine with thread to match the fabric patches or with threads that coordinate or contrast with fabrics. Rayon thread is a good choice when a sheen is desired on the finished appliqué stitches. Do not use rayon thread in the bobbin; use all-purpose thread.

When all machine work is complete, remove stabilizer from the back referring to the manufacturer's instructions.

Putting It All Together

Finishing the Top

Settings. Most quilts are made by sewing individual blocks together in rows that, when joined, create a design. There are several other methods used to join blocks. Sometimes the setting choice is determined by the block's design. For example, a House block should be placed upright on a quilt, not sideways or upside down.

Plain blocks can be alternated with pieced or appliquéd blocks in a straight set. Making a quilt using plain blocks saves time; half the number of pieced or appliquéd blocks are needed to make the same-size quilt as shown in Figure 1.

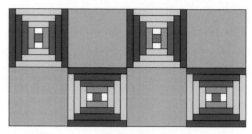

Figure 1
Alternate plain blocks with pieced blocks to save time.

Adding Borders. Borders are an integral part of the quilt and should complement the colors and designs used in the quilt center. Borders frame a quilt just like a mat and frame do a picture.

If fabric strips are added for borders, they may be mitered or butted at the corners as shown in Figures 2 and 3. To determine the size for butted border strips, measure across the center of the completed quilt top from one side raw edge to the other side raw edge. This measurement will include a ¼" seam allowance.

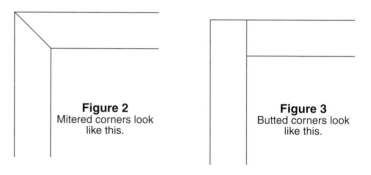

Figure 2
Mitered corners look
like this.

Figure 3
Butted corners look
like this.

Cut two border strips that length by the chosen width of the border. Sew these strips to the top and bottom of the pieced center referring to Figure 4. Press the seam allowance toward the border strips.

Figure 4
Sew border strips to
opposite sides; sew
remaining 2 strips to
remaining sides to make
butted corners.

Measure across the completed quilt top at the center, from top raw edge to bottom raw edge, including the two border strips already added. Cut two border strips that length by the chosen width of the border. Sew a strip to each of the two remaining sides as shown in Figure 4. Press the seams toward the border strips.

To make mitered corners, measure the quilt as before. To this add twice the width of the border and ½" for seam allowances to determine the length of the strips. Repeat for opposite sides. Sew on each strip, stopping stitching ¼" from corner, leaving the remainder of the strip dangling.

Press corners at a 45-degree angle to form a crease. Stitch from the inside quilt corner to the outside on the creased line. Trim excess away after stitching and press mitered seams open (Figures 5–7).

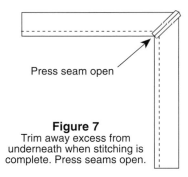

Press seam open

Figure 7
Trim away excess from underneath when stitching is complete. Press seams open.

Carefully press the entire piece, including the pieced center. Avoid pulling and stretching while pressing, which would distort shapes.

Getting Ready to Quilt

Choosing a Quilting Design. If you choose to hand- or machine-quilt your finished top, you will need to select a design for quilting.

There are several types of quilting designs, some of which may not have to be marked. The easiest of the unmarked designs is in-the-ditch quilting. Here the quilting stitches are placed in the valley created by the seams joining two pieces together or next to the edge of an appliqué design. There is no need to mark a top for in-the-ditch quilting. Machine quilters choose this option because the stitches are not as obvious on the finished quilt. (Figure 8).

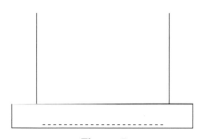

Figure 5
For mitered corner, stitch strip, stopping 1/4" from corner seam.

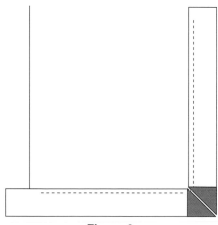

Figure 6
Fold and press corner to make a 45-degree angle.

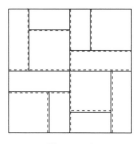

Figure 8
In-the-ditch quilting is done in the seam that joins 2 pieces.

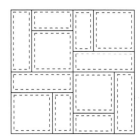

Figure 9
Outline-quilting 1/4" away from seam is a popular choice for quilting.

Outline-quilting ¼" or more away from seams or appliqué shapes is another no-mark alternative (Figure 9) that prevents having to sew through the layers made by seams, thus making stitching easier.

General Instructions

If you are not comfortable eyeballing the ¼" (or other distance), masking tape is available in different widths and is helpful to place on straight-edge designs to mark the quilting line. If using masking tape, place the tape right up against the seam and quilt close to the other edge.

Meander or free-motion quilting by machine fills in open spaces and doesn't require marking. It is fun and easy to stitch as shown in Figure 10.

Figure 10
Machine meander quilting fills in large spaces.

Marking the Top for Quilting. If you choose a fancy or allover design for quilting, you will need to transfer the design to your quilt top before layering with the backing and batting. You may use a sharp medium-lead or silver pencil on light background fabrics. Test the pencil marks to guarantee that they will wash out of your quilt top when quilting is complete; or be sure your quilting stitches cover the pencil marks. Mechanical pencils with very fine points may be used successfully to mark quilts.

Manufactured quilt-design templates are available in many designs and sizes and are cut out of a durable plastic template material that is easy to use.

To make a permanent quilt-design template, choose a template material on which to transfer the design. See-through plastic is the best as it will let you place the design while allowing you to see where it is in relation to your quilt design without moving it. Place the design on the quilt top where you want it and trace around it with your marking tool. Pick up the quilting template and place again; repeat marking.

No matter what marking method you use, remember—the marked lines should never show on the finished quilt. When the top is marked, it is ready for layering.

Preparing the Quilt Backing. The quilt backing is a very important feature of your quilt. The materials listed for each quilt in this book includes the size requirements for the backing, not the yardage needed. Exceptions to this are when the backing fabric is also used on the quilt top and yardage is given for that fabric.

A backing is generally cut at least 4" larger than the quilt top or 2" larger on all sides. For a 64" x 78" finished quilt, the backing would need to be at least 68" x 82".

To avoid having the seam across the center of the quilt backing, cut or tear one of the right-length pieces in half and sew half to each side of the second piece as shown in Figure 11.

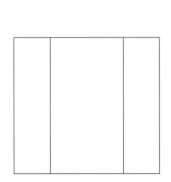

Figure 11
Center 1 backing piece with a piece on each side.

Figure 12
Horizontal seams may be used on backing pieces.

Quilts that need a backing more than 88" wide may be pieced in horizontal pieces as shown in Figure 12.

Layering the Quilt Sandwich. Layering the quilt top with the batting and backing is time-consuming. Open the batting several days before you need it and place over a bed or flat on the floor to help flatten the creases caused from its being folded up in the bag for so long.

Iron the backing piece, folding in half both vertically and horizontally and pressing to mark centers.

If you will not be quilting on a frame, place the backing right side down on a clean floor or table. Start in the center and push any wrinkles or bunches flat. Use masking tape to tape the edges to the floor or large clips to hold the backing to the edges of the table. The backing should be taut.

Place the batting on top of the backing, matching centers using fold lines as guides; flatten out any wrinkles. Trim the batting to the same size as the backing.

Fold the quilt top in half lengthwise and place on top of the batting, wrong side against the batting, matching centers. Unfold quilt and, working from the center to the outside edges, smooth out any wrinkles or lumps.

To hold the quilt layers together for quilting, baste by hand or use safety pins. If basting by hand, thread a long thin needle with a long piece of unknotted white or off-white thread. Starting in the center and leaving a long tail, make 4"–6" stitches toward the outside edge of the quilt top, smoothing as you baste. Start at the center again and work toward the outside as shown in Figure 13.

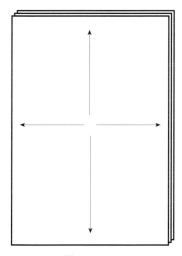

Figure 13
Baste from the center to the outside edges.

If quilting by machine, you may prefer to use safety pins for holding your fabric sandwich together. Start in the center of the quilt and pin to the outside, leaving pins open until all are placed. When you are satisfied that all layers are smooth, close the pins.

Quilting

Hand Quilting. Hand quilting is the process of placing stitches through the quilt top, batting and backing to hold them together. While it is a functional process, it also adds beauty and loft to the finished quilt.

To begin, thread a sharp between needle with an 18" piece of quilting thread. Tie a small knot in the end of the thread. Position the needle about ½" to 1" away from the starting point on quilt top. Sink the needle through the top into the batting layer but not through the backing. Pull the needle up at the starting point

of the quilting design. Pull the needle and thread until the knot sinks through the top into the batting (Figure 14).

Figure 14
Start the needle through the top layer of fabric 1/2"–1"
away from quilting line with knot on top of fabric.

Some stitchers like to take a backstitch here at the beginning while others prefer to begin the first stitch here. Take small, even running stitches along the marked quilting line (Figure 15). Keep one hand positioned underneath to feel the needle go all the way through to the backing.

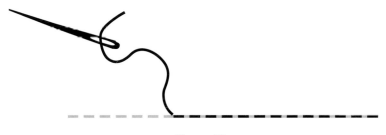

Figure 15
Make small, even running stitches on marked quilting line.

When you have nearly run out of thread, wind the thread around the needle several times to make a small knot and pull it close to the fabric. Insert the needle into the fabric on the quilting line and come out with the needle ½" to 1" away, pulling the knot into the fabric layers the same as when you started. Pull and cut thread close to fabric. The end should disappear inside after cutting. Some quilters prefer to take a backstitch with a loop through it for a knot to end.

Machine Quilting. Successful machine quilting requires practice and a good relationship with your sewing machine.

Prepare the quilt for machine quilting in the same way as for hand quilting. Use safety pins to hold the layers together instead of basting with thread.

Presser-foot quilting is best used for straight-line quilting because the presser bar lever does not need to be continually lifted.

Set the machine on a longer stitch length (3.0 or 8–10 stitches to the inch). Too tight a stitch causes puckering and fabric

General Instructions

tucks, either on the quilt top or backing. An even-feed or walking foot helps to eliminate the tucks and puckering by feeding the upper and lower layers through the machine evenly. Before you begin, loosen the amount of pressure on the presser foot.

Special machine-quilting needles work best to penetrate the three layers in your quilt.

Decide on a design. Quilting in the ditch is not quite as visible, but if you quilt with the feed dogs engaged, it means turning the quilt frequently. It is not easy to fit a rolled-up quilt through the small opening on the sewing machine head.

Meander quilting is the easiest way to machine-quilt—and it is fun. Meander quilting is done using an appliqué or darning foot with the feed dogs dropped. It is sort of like scribbling. Simply move the quilt top around under the foot and make stitches in a random pattern to fill the space. The same method may be used to outline a quilt design. The trick is the same as in hand quilting; you are striving for stitches of uniform size. Your hands are in complete control of the design.

If machine quilting is of interest to you, there are several very good books available at quilt shops that will help you become a successful machine quilter.

Finishing the Edges

After your quilt is tied or quilted, the edges need to be finished. Decide how you want the edges of your quilt finished before layering the backing and batting with the quilt top.

Without Binding—Self-Finish. There is one way to eliminate adding an edge finish. This is done before quilting. Place the batting on a flat surface. Place the pieced top right side up on the batting. Place the backing right sides together with the pieced top. Pin and/or baste the layers together to hold flat referring to Layering the Quilt Sandwich.

Begin stitching in the center of one side using a ¼" seam allowance, reversing at the beginning and end of the seam. Continue stitching all around and back to the beginning side. Leave a 12" or larger opening. Clip corners to reduce excess. Turn right side out through the opening. Slipstitch the opening closed by hand. The quilt may now be quilted by hand or machine.

The disadvantage to this method is that once the edges are sewn in, any creases or wrinkles that might form during the quilting process cannot be flattened out. Tying is the preferred method for finishing a quilt constructed using this method.

Bringing the backing fabric to the front is another way to finish the quilt's edge without binding. To accomplish this, complete the quilt as for hand or machine quilting. Trim the batting only even with the front. Trim the backing 1" larger than the completed top all around.

Turn the backing edge in ½" and then turn over to the front along edge of batting. The folded edge may be machine-stitched close to the edge through all layers, or blind-stitched in place to finish.

The front may be turned to the back. If using this method, a wider front border is needed. The backing and batting are trimmed 1" smaller than the top and the top edge is turned under 1/2" and then turned to the back and stitched in place.

One more method of self-finish may be used. The top and backing may be stitched together by hand at the edge. To accomplish this, all quilting must be stopped ½" from the quilt-top edge. The top and backing of the quilt are trimmed even and the batting is trimmed to ¼"–½" smaller. The edges of the top and backing are turned in ¼"–½" and blind-stitched together at the very edge.

These methods do not require the use of extra fabric and save time in preparation of binding strips; they are not as durable as an added binding.

Binding. The technique of adding extra fabric at the edges of the quilt is called binding. The binding encloses the edges and adds an extra layer of fabric for durability.

To prepare the quilt for the addition of the binding, trim the batting and backing layers flush with the top of the quilt using a rotary cutter and ruler or shears. Using a walking-foot attachment (sometimes called an even-feed foot attachment), machine-baste the three layers together all around approximately ⅛" from the cut edge.

The materials listed for each quilt in this book often includes a number of yards of self-made or purchased binding. Bias binding may be purchased in packages and in many colors. The advantage to self-made binding is that you can use fabrics from your quilt to coordinate colors. Double-fold, straight-grain binding and double fold, bias-grain binding are two of the most commonly used types of binding.

Double-fold, straight-grain binding is used on smaller projects with right-angle corners. Double-fold, bias-grain binding is best suited for bed-size quilts or quilts with rounded corners.

To make double-fold, straight-grain binding, cut 2¼"-wide strips of fabric across the width or down the length of the fabric totaling the perimeter of the quilt plus 10". The strips are joined as shown in Figure 16 and pressed in half wrong sides together along the length using an iron on a cotton setting with no steam.

Figure 16
Join binding strips in a diagonal seam to eliminate bulk as shown.

Lining up the raw edges, place the binding on the top of the quilt and begin sewing (again using the walking foot) approximately 6" from the beginning of the binding strip. Stop sewing ¼" from the first corner, leave the needle in the quilt, turn and sew diagonally to the corner as shown in Figure 17.

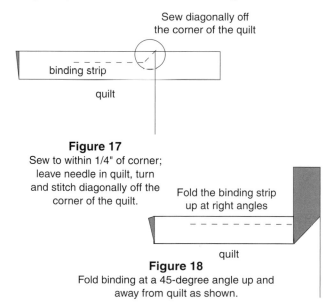

Sew diagonally off the corner of the quilt

binding strip

quilt

Figure 17
Sew to within 1/4" of corner; leave needle in quilt, turn and stitch diagonally off the corner of the quilt.

Fold the binding strip up at right angles

quilt

Figure 18
Fold binding at a 45-degree angle up and away from quilt as shown.

Fold the binding at a 45-degree angle up and away from the quilt as shown in Figure 18 and back down flush with the raw edges. Starting at the top raw edge of the quilt, begin sewing the next side as shown in Figure 19. Repeat at the next three corners.

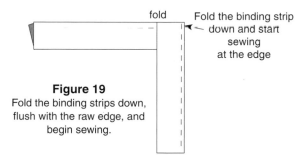

fold   Fold the binding strip
             down and start
             sewing
             at the edge

Figure 19
Fold the binding strips down, flush with the raw edge, and begin sewing.

As you approach the beginning of the binding strip, stop stitching and overlap the binding ½" from the edge; trim. Join the two ends with a ¼" seam allowance and press the seam open. Reposition the joined binding along the edge of the quilt and resume stitching to the beginning.

To finish, bring the folded edge of the binding over the raw edges and blind-stitch the binding in place over the machine-stitching line on the backside. Hand-miter the corners on the back as shown in Figure 20.

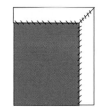

Figure 20
Miter and stitch the corners as shown.

If you are making a quilt to be used on a bed, you may want to use double-fold, bias-grain bindings because the many threads that cross each other along the fold at the edge of the quilt make it a more durable binding.

Cut 2¼"-wide bias strips from a large square of fabric. Join the strips as illustrated in Figure 16 and press the seams open. Fold the beginning end of the bias strip ¼" from the raw edge and press. Fold the joined strips in half along the long side, wrong sides together, and press with no steam (Figure 21).

Figure 21
Fold and press strip in half.

Follow the same procedures as previously described for preparing the quilt top and sewing the binding to the quilt top. Treat the corners just as you treated them with straight-grain binding.

Since you are using bias-grain binding, you do have the option to just eliminate the corners if this option doesn't interfere with the patchwork in the quilt. Round the corners off by

General Instructions

placing one of your dinner plates at the corner and rotary-cutting the gentle curve (Figure 22).

As you approach the beginning of the binding strip, stop stitching and lay the end across the beginning so it will slip inside the fold. Cut the end at a 45-degree angle so the raw edges are contained inside the beginning of the strip (Figure 23). Resume stitching to the beginning. Bring the fold to the back of the quilt and hand-stitch as previously described.

Figure 22
Round corners to eliminate square-corner finishes.

Figure 23
End the binding strips as shown.

Overlapped corners are not quite as easy as rounded ones, but a bit easier than mitering. To make overlapped corners, sew binding strips to opposite sides of the quilt top. Stitch edges down to finish. Trim ends even.

Sew a strip to each remaining side, leaving 1½"–2" excess at each end. Turn quilt over and fold binding down even with previous finished edge as shown in Figure 24.

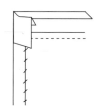

Figure 24
Fold end of binding even with previous page.

Figure 25
An overlapped corner is not quite as neat as a mitered corner.

Fold binding in toward quilt and stitch down as before, enclosing the previous bound edge in the seam as shown in Figure 25. It may be necessary to trim the folded-down section to reduce bulk.

Final Touches

If your quilt will be hung on the wall, a hanging sleeve is required. Other options include purchased plastic rings or fabric tabs. The best choice is a fabric sleeve, which will evenly distribute the weight of the quilt across the top edge, rather than at selected spots where tabs or rings are stitched, keep the quilt hanging straight and not damage the batting.

To make a sleeve, measure across the top of the finished quilt. Cut an 8"-wide piece of muslin equal to that length—you may need to seam several muslin strips together to make the required length.

Fold in ¼" on each end of the muslin strip and press. Fold again and stitch to hold. Fold the muslin strip lengthwise with right sides together. Sew along the long side to make a tube. Turn the tube right side out; press with seam at bottom or centered on the back.

Hand-stitch the tube along the top of the quilt and the bottom of the tube to the quilt back making sure the quilt lies flat. Stitches should not go through to the front of the quilt and don't need to be too close together as shown in Figure 26.

Slip a wooden dowel or long curtain rod through the sleeve to hang.

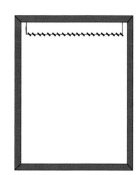

Figure 26
Sew a sleeve to the top back of the quilt.

When the quilt is finally complete, it should be signed and dated. Use a permanent pen on the back of the quilt. Other methods include cross-stitching your name and date on the front or back or making a permanent label which may be stitched to the back.